The Writer's Life Planning Guide

© Copyright 2022
by Melinda Kiker & Jennifer Kochert

All rights reserved. This book or any portion thereof may not be reproduced or used in any manner whatsoever without the express written permission of the publisher except for the use of brief quotations.

Flourish Ministries LLC
FlourishWriters.com

Unless otherwise marked, Scripture quotations are from The Holy Bible,
New International Version® NIV®. Copyright © 1973, 1978, 1984 by International Bible Society®.
Used by permission. All rights reserved worldwide.

Scripture quotations marked MSG are from The Message.
Copyright © 1993, 1994, 1995, 1996, 2000, 2001, 2002 by Eugene H. Peterson.
Used by permission of NavPress, represented by Tyndale House Publishers. All rights reserved.

Scripture quotations marked TPT are from The Passion Translation®. Copyright © 2017, 2018
by Passion & Fire Ministries, Inc. Used by permission. All rights reserved. ThePassionTranslation.com.

Scripture quotations marked ESV are from the ESV® Bible (The Holy Bible, English Standard Version®).
Copyright © 2001 by Crossway Bibles, a publishing ministry of Good News Publishers.
Used by permission. All rights reserved.

Scripture quotations marked NASB are from the New American Standard Bible®.
Copyright © 1960, 1962, 1963, 1968, 1971, 1972, 1973, 1975, 1977, 1995
by The Lockman Foundation. Used by permission. www.lockman.org.

Cover and layout design by Nelly Murariu at PixBeeDesign.com

Welcome

We're thrilled you're here to make bold strides in your writing journey this year. What fun we're going to have making history together.

You did a big thing. You took a courageous step to join us. So how are you feeling about it now? Excited? Afraid? Intimidated? You might be floating on a cloud, thrilled at the prospect of making steady progress in your writing life this year. Or you're wondering if you made the right choice. Was this a good idea?

We think you made a brilliant choice. Of course, we may be biased, but we also know what writers need, both from our own experience and from serving our writing community.

Doubt and uncertainty are familiar voices in a writer's head. This year, you'll learn to put them in their place. You'll also grow in your craft and bolster those places of weakness. You're in good company. FlourishWriters is here to encourage and equip you. We cultivate an atmosphere of honor and a can-do spirit.

We're excited about your commitment to take your writing seriously, set goals, and work toward them consistently. Perhaps you struggled to carve out writing time in the past, because you didn't have a support structure in place to help you succeed. Now you do.

You're going to love *The Writer's Life Planning Guide*. With the clarity it will help you gain on your writing goals, you'll enjoy sitting down to write confident in where you're headed, focusing on the right thing at the right time.

Your presence here is a significant step into your dreams of blessing others with your words. We help writers come to life. It's a calling we love.

Be encouraged by words from Paul: *I run straight for the divine invitation of reaching the heavenly goal and gaining the victory-prize through the anointing of Jesus* (Philippians 3:14 TPT).

We can't wait to see you with that victory prize.

Here's to flourishing in your writing life, one story at a time!

Jenny and Mindy

FlourishWriters believe in the power of their story, a *declaration* of hope to this generation.

They cultivate the courage to *dream*, *write*, and *publish* the story inside.

Their words shout, *Freedom*.

Their heart calls out, *Dream again*.

Their message proclaims, *God is good*.

FlourishWriters step out boldly and say *Yes* a thousand times to God's call.

Contents

Meet Your Mentors — 4

THE WRITER'S LIFE PLANNING GUIDE — 7

How Does the Planning Guide Work? — 8
Creating a Vision for Your Writing Journey — 9
Evaluate and Reflect: Your Writing Life — 10
"I Am a FlourishWriter": Scripture and Affirmation — 13
Create the Vision — 14
Write a Vision Statement — 16
Translate Vision into Goals — 17
Brainstorm Your Goals — 18
Choose Your Goals — 20
Plan Your Goals — 21
Finalize a Plan for Your Writing Life — 26

THE WRITER'S LIFE QUARTERLY PLANNING — 29

The First Quarter (January, February, March) — 30
First Quarter in Review — 76
The Second Quarter (April, May, June) — 80
Second Quarter in Review — 126
The Third Quarter (July, August, September) — 130
Third Quarter in Review — 176
The Fourth Quarter (October, November, December) — 180
Fourth Quarter in Review — 226

THE WRITER'S LIFE YEAR IN REVIEW — 229

THE WRITER'S BLOCK REMEDY KIT — 235

Meet Your Mentors

When we started our writing journey, we had a vision, but we weren't sure how to pursue it. We were confident in the calling, and we knew it would take trust and obedience, but we also had to figure out how to move forward. First we had to figure out what questions to ask. We. Knew. Precious. Little. But we knew the One who would guide us.

We also had each other. Companionship gets you through hard times, confusion, self-doubt, and despair. When one of us wanted to give up, the other rushed in with support.

We started Flourish by writing our stories. We wanted to encourage women to grow in God's Word, to see Jesus show up in everyday life.

FlourishWriters came into being to answer the requests we received from readers: "We love the passion in your writing. We love your studies. Can you teach us how you do it?"

Since we're systems thinkers who naturally simplify difficult tasks into a step-by-step process, we started sharing what we know: how to write, publish, and cultivate community.

We launched FlourishWriters in 2018. We've been thrilled to help thousands of writers—some writing for the first time— as they plan, organize, and write their personal stories that testify of God's faithfulness.

FlourishWriters has taken on a life of its own as the community has grown. We create online conferences and writer's retreats, as well as training courses to address the needs of writers at each stage of the writing journey. Our mission is to support aspiring and working writers with practical how-to guidance and nurture for the writer's heart, helping you flourish one story at a time.

The FlourishWriters Academy is our gift of friendship to our students. It's what we wanted when we started writing. But we couldn't find it, so we created it.

We daily encounter writers who desire to pursue their calling, but they're exhausted by jumping the hurdles alone, no coach and no training partners in view. It breaks our hearts, because this does not need to be a writer's story.

That is not your story. No, indeed. You're here making history with us at FlourishWriters.

Jennifer Kochert and **Mindy Kiker** are passionate about helping writers grow in God's Word. For those desiring to share their God stories in writing, they are guides who help birth messages from the heart to the page. The Lord has put a story on their lips and a passion in their hearts to encourage you to flourish in your writing life.

Jenny inspires the Flourish community by opening her life and God's Word to reveal practical ways to walk with Jesus. If you listen closely, you'll hear Jenny's Cuban heritage as she relates stories of growing up in Miami, joining her dad as a private investigator, and running her own PI firm for nine years. With a master's degree in entrepreneurship from the University of Florida, she believes in the power of an online community as a gathering place to cultivate transformation and growth. Jenny lives with her husband, Ryan, and daughter, Sophia, in central Kentucky, where they serve in ministry as a family.

Mindy grew up making sandcastles by the sea, dancing the hula in Hawaii, and singing Zulu songs in South Africa. She enjoys drawing readers close to God's heart, where His love meets them with healing and freedom. Mindy's passion for seeing people grow was energized over a decade in South Africa, where she worked in adult education, community development, and entrepreneurship. With a BA in English and linguistics from the University of Florida and an MSc in organizational and leadership systems from the University of KwaZulu-Natal, she lends her expertise to building a learning community online. Mindy makes her home in Florida with her husband and four sons.

The Writer's Life *Planning* Guide

Clarity and vision are key to thriving in your writing life. You've heard it's possible, and you've experienced it at times, but you may find it challenging to sustain.

When you're doing *all the things* but still feeling stuck, when the goal so clear last month is confusing now, you need a process to help clarify your vision and stay focused, to do the right thing at the right time and make forward progress.

We don't want you to plan and make decisions only to second-guess yourself and become sidetracked, never quite getting around to the projects that matter.

Flourishing doesn't suddenly appear in your writing life after just one workshop or one planning session. It builds as you develop the right habits over months of cultivated growth. The purpose of *The Writer's Life Planning Guide* is to help you put a plan in place and keep your priorities clear.

Many writers languish before they find their beat, because they expect instant growth. Slow and steady wins the race, but even slow and steady needs to be headed in the right direction. How do you know where you're going?

The Writer's Life Planning Guide is designed to help you clarify your vision, set goals, take action, and evaluate progress, so you can make adjustments as your writing journey unfolds. We want you to see long-term growth, not the fast dash of the hare, but the way of the tortoise—one determined step at a time.

By focusing on true transformation, you find what works for your situation and your unique goals, curating the components of a robust and sustainable writing journey.

It's time to dig into your planning guide. We pray you experience the benefits of having a plan based on a Spirit-breathed vision for your writing life. Let's tend your garden so you can create a year to flourish that yields a bountiful harvest.

How Does the *Planning* Guide Work?

The *Writer's Life Planning Guide* provides a simple process to help you clarify your writing life in the context of your personal life. Clarity comes from establishing an overall vision for the year and complementary visions for each quarter, month, and week. We make it easy for you to define the target and keep your eyes on the goal.

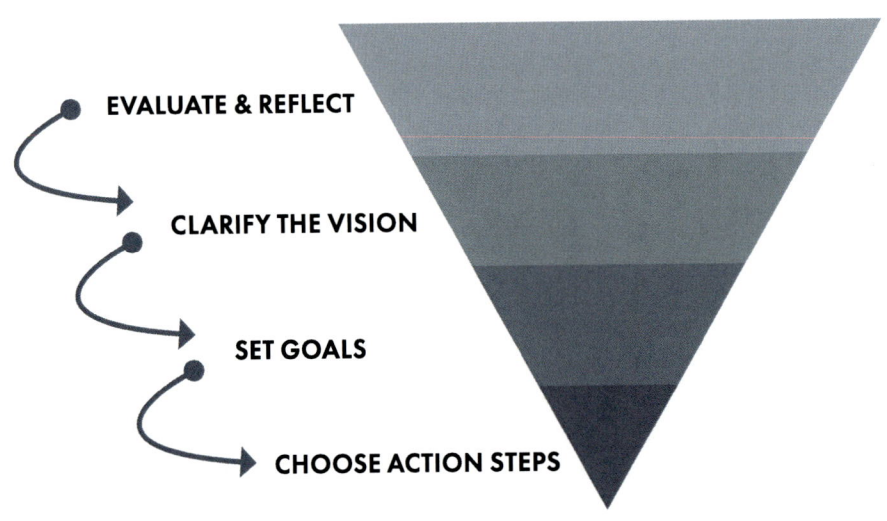

We begin the planning process by creating a vision for your writing journey. Planning is not reserved for January alone. Wherever you are in the year, you can begin thinking about the next twelve months.

Using your vision for the year, you plan the first quarter to clarify your focus for the next 90 days. From that place of clarity, you set goals and then choose your action steps.

When you have your plan for the first quarter clearly in mind, you follow the same process to plan for the first month, by setting your key focus, goals, and action steps. Once you translate this approach to weekly and daily plans, you're on your way.

Don't be intimidated by this process. *The Writer's Life Planning Guide* guides you step-by-step. As you stay committed to following the process, you will discover that small-yet-purposeful steps will help you achieve writing goals. Even if you've been frustrated in the past, we encourage you to keep showing up, and you'll enter a new season of abundance in your writing life.

Creating a *Vision* for Your Writing Journey

For many years, I (Jenny) was afraid to evaluate my life. I thought my frustrations, worries, and concerns came from a lack of faith. Maybe I wasn't doing something right, or I was lazy, or I wasn't making good decisions, or I was simply ungrateful. I would try harder to figure it out. I felt ashamed that I was consumed by worries.

A few years ago, the Lord spoke to me during one of my worry sessions and explained that frustrations are His merciful warning beacons. My emotions are from Him. I don't have to hide or pretend I have it all together. I can bring my concerns to God.

That insight began to change everything. As soon as I felt the rumbling of frustration—the feeling that change was needed—I would immediately run to Jesus and ask Him about it. I did this through journaling, pouring my heart out to the Lord, telling Him how I feel, describing my worries, concerns, and desires.

I asked the Lord to speak to me. He sifted through my concerns with His grace and His will for my life. I was left with peace, clarity, encouragement, and direction.

At FlourishWriters, we refer to peaceful, clear direction as "vision."

Be encouraged. Even if you don't consider yourself a dreamer, a visionary, or a planner, we desire to see you move forward with confidence. We're going to dream together about what this year can look like.

Vision **guides** us by revealing which projects to put our energies into and which to let go.

It **illuminates** and clarifies, so we stay focused on what we aim to do in this season.

It **reveals** where we're going, so we don't waste time walking down a dead-end path.

It **helps** us make decisions, so we don't jump for good ideas rather than waiting for God ideas.

It **protects** us with boundaries, so we don't get confused by other people's opinions, fall into the comparison trap, or become exhausted chasing shiny objects.

As you begin your journey, your starting place is to reflect on and evaluate your writing life. Once you've reflected on your current situation and evaluated where you are, you'll create your vision for the year. Enjoy the process.

Evaluate *and* Reflect: Your Writing Life

Let's take a moment of reflection. Don't overthink these questions. Write what first comes to mind. You'll continue to mull over these questions, and you can come back and add additional insights later.

What's going well in my writing life right now?

What am I thankful for?

What brings me energy and joy?

Where did I get off track in my writing life during the last year?

What frustrations did I experience?

What remains puzzling or complicated as I think about the next year?

What changes would I like to make as I move forward?

What do I desire to see in my writing life?

Scripture

What Bible verse expresses your hopes for your writing life this year? Write it on the next page.

Affirmation

What do you hope for your writing life this year? Craft a prayer to declare over yourself every time you sit down to write.

"I AM A Flourish WRITER"

Scripture

Affirmation

Create the Vision

Now you're moving on from evaluating and reflecting to creating a vision for your year. If you feel blocked or stalled out at any stage, stop and pray. Dig into *The Writer's Block Remedy Kit* at the end of this guide. The kit's spiritual battle plan and soul-care remedies will guide you through times of overwhelm and blocked creativity and help you find joy and peace.

As you process the insights from the "Evaluate and Reflect" section you just completed, ask yourself, "What are the priorities in my writing life?" and "Why are they important to me?"

Perhaps you have a project on your heart. Or perhaps you desire to be more intentional in your writing life but aren't sure where to start. Use the space on the next page to brainstorm the priorities you may pursue this year, without the pressure of choosing your direction just yet. When we get into goal setting, you can get more specific about where you'll start.

What are the priorities in my writing life?

Why are they important to me?

Write a *Vision* Statement

As you ponder the priorities in your writing life and why they are important to you, you're getting at the heart of your vision. God designed you with a unique purpose and a distinctive calling on your life. It is no accident you were born into this generation, into your family and community. It's no coincidence you're here at FlourishWriters with a desire to grow in your writing life. You are a vital part of the kingdom of God, and when you function within your gifting, you shine as a brilliant light in a dark and confused world.

God created us with a passion for vision, to know where we're going and what we're called to accomplish. Vision provides strength and energy. It's what we return to when we become lost along the way. We break free into a fruitful writing life when guided by a vision inspired by Holy Spirit.

Use the space below to describe your vision for the message God has written on the pages of your life. Your vision is your why. It's the purpose that motivates you to do what you do. Vision answers questions like:

- Why is this work important to me?
- Why do I want to spend my time and energy doing this?
- What transformation do I want to see in people's lives?

Once you establish your vision, goals are the projects you work on to achieve the vision. The vision is the why, the goals are the what, and the action steps are the how.

Our vision statement at FlourishWriters is to encourage and equip communicators to tell their God stories. We are midwives who help writers birth messages from the heart to the page.

VISION STATEMENT

Translate Vision into *Goals*

Great job! You're getting closer to having a working vision translated into goals and action steps. You've progressed from evaluating and reflecting on the big picture of your writing life, to clarifying your vision, and now to goal setting. It's getting real.

A word of caution about the goal-setting process: when we seek perfection rather than growth, we set ourselves up for trouble. Perfection creates paralysis. It makes us want to give up if we can't do something perfectly the first time. Focusing on growth reveals opportunity. It helps us keep moving forward, responding to roadblocks with curiosity and a desire to adapt. Failure is not a disaster but, rather, a natural part of learning.

We want to set achievable goals that can be turned into doable action steps. If we stop the planning process too soon, we have a big vision with lofty, vague goals that are too far off in the future.

When vision is not translated into goals and then action steps, you're set up for frustration. *The Writer's Life Planning Guide* is designed to help you find clarity, so you're headed in the right direction. Goals establish a destination on a map. Action steps are the directions that get you there.

The Scripture below is a favorite of ours and is our declaration over you. We encourage you to declare it over yourself out loud by inserting your name in the passage.

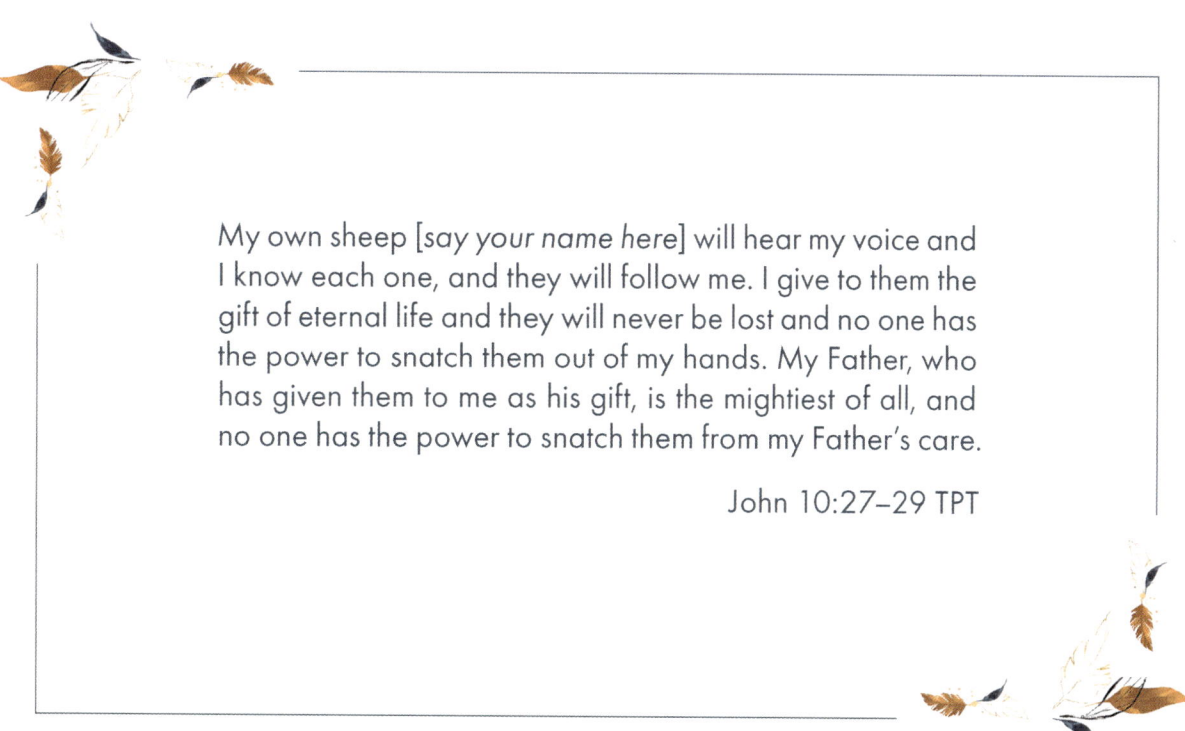

My own sheep [*say your name here*] will hear my voice and I know each one, and they will follow me. I give to them the gift of eternal life and they will never be lost and no one has the power to snatch them out of my hands. My Father, who has given them to me as his gift, is the mightiest of all, and no one has the power to snatch them from my Father's care.

John 10:27–29 TPT

Brainstorm Your Goals

Identifying your goals helps you determine your direction and destination for the year. Goal setting establishes a boundary so you know which activities to accept and which to decline.

Visualize an archer aiming at a bull's-eye. That is a picture of goal setting: seeing the target, knowing your purpose, and mustering concentrated intent to achieve the objective.

Aimlessness is the fate of those who don't set goals. Burnout is another by-product of trying to navigate without choosing appropriate goals for your current season. It's unwise to load up your already busy life with more to-dos. Adding on that new project may be the proverbial straw that breaks the camel's back. When you plan, you look at the whole picture and see what you need to let go of before grabbing hold of something new.

On the next page, you have space to brainstorm your goal ideas. Look back at the priorities you identified earlier and spend as much time as you need brainstorming your potential goals for the next year.

You may not be sure about the feasibility of an idea. Is it too big or too much to take on right now? If the idea is in line with your vision, write it down as a potential goal, then give yourself a month or two to figure it out.

If you get stalled in the brainstorm, remember that goals do not need to be perfect. Make provisional decisions and move on to the next steps. This planning process has ample opportunities for you to revise and adjust any goals that aren't working.

Brainstorm Goal Ideas

Choose Your Goals

After all that reflecting and brainstorming, you're ready to nail down your writing goal(s). We provide space here for you to write three, but you do not need to have three goals. You may have only one or two. If you have many goals, we suggest you narrow them down for the time being. We encourage you to be focused rather than scattered.

Write each goal by starting with an action word (a verb), as in "write my book," "start my blog," "publish my Bible study," and so on.

GOAL 1

GOAL 2

GOAL 3

Plan Your Goals

The next step is to plan your goals by thinking through what may be needed to accomplish each one. This step helps you understand each goal so you're set up for quarterly and monthly planning. You might want to begin with sticky notes or work in a journal or on a big piece of paper. Use whatever planning approach is most familiar to you. The following questions may help you flesh out each goal:

- What **resources** do I need to accomplish this goal?

- What **support** do I need?

- What **people** do I need?

- What do I **need to learn**?

After you get all your thoughts onto sticky notes or in your journal, transfer your main ideas to a goal-planning map on the following pages.

Make one map for each goal. Write each goal in a map's center circle, then fill in the outer circles.

Review the example goal-planning map to give you an idea of what you're aiming for.

EXAMPLE GOAL-PLANNING MAP

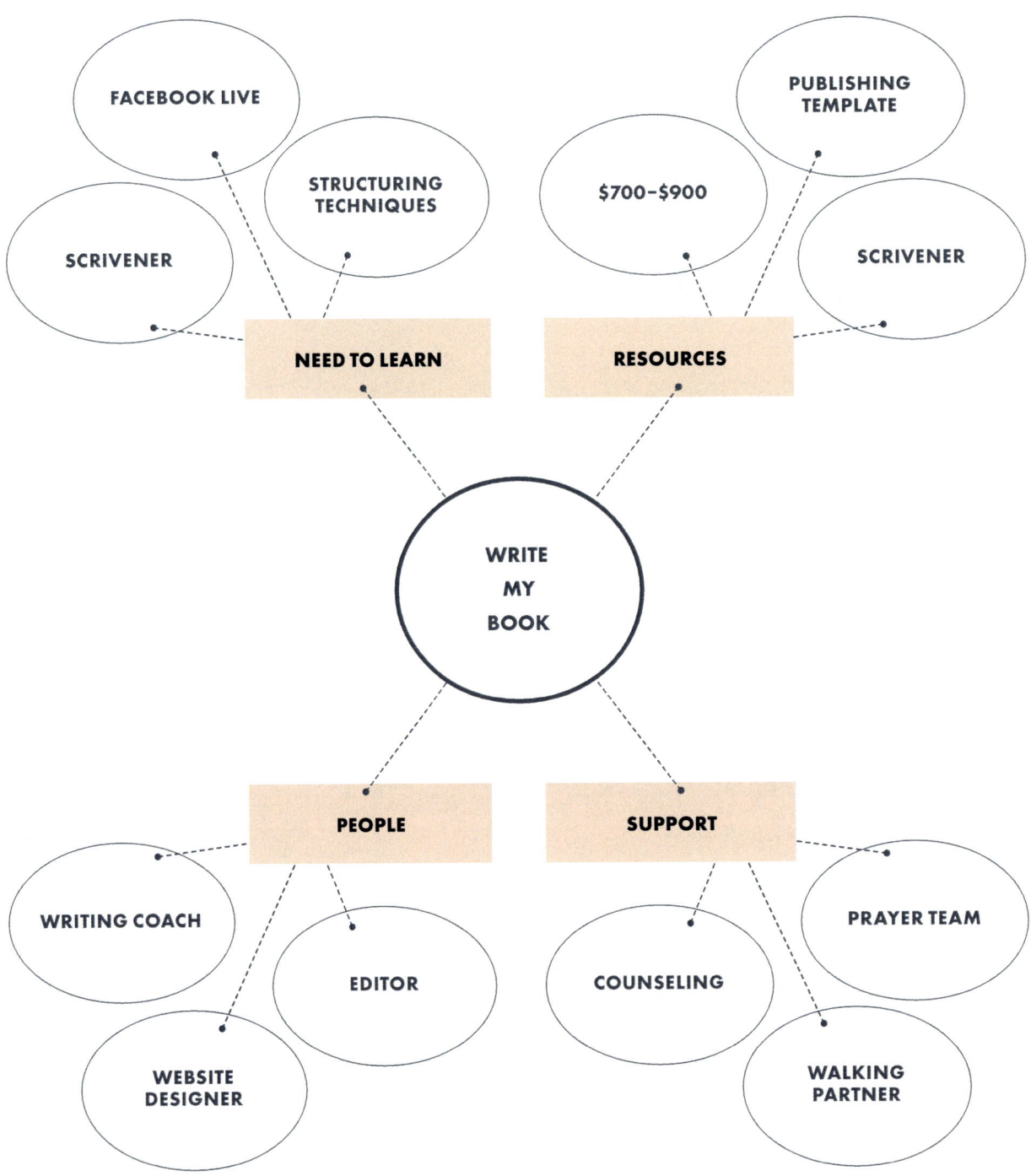

GOAL-PLANNING MAP

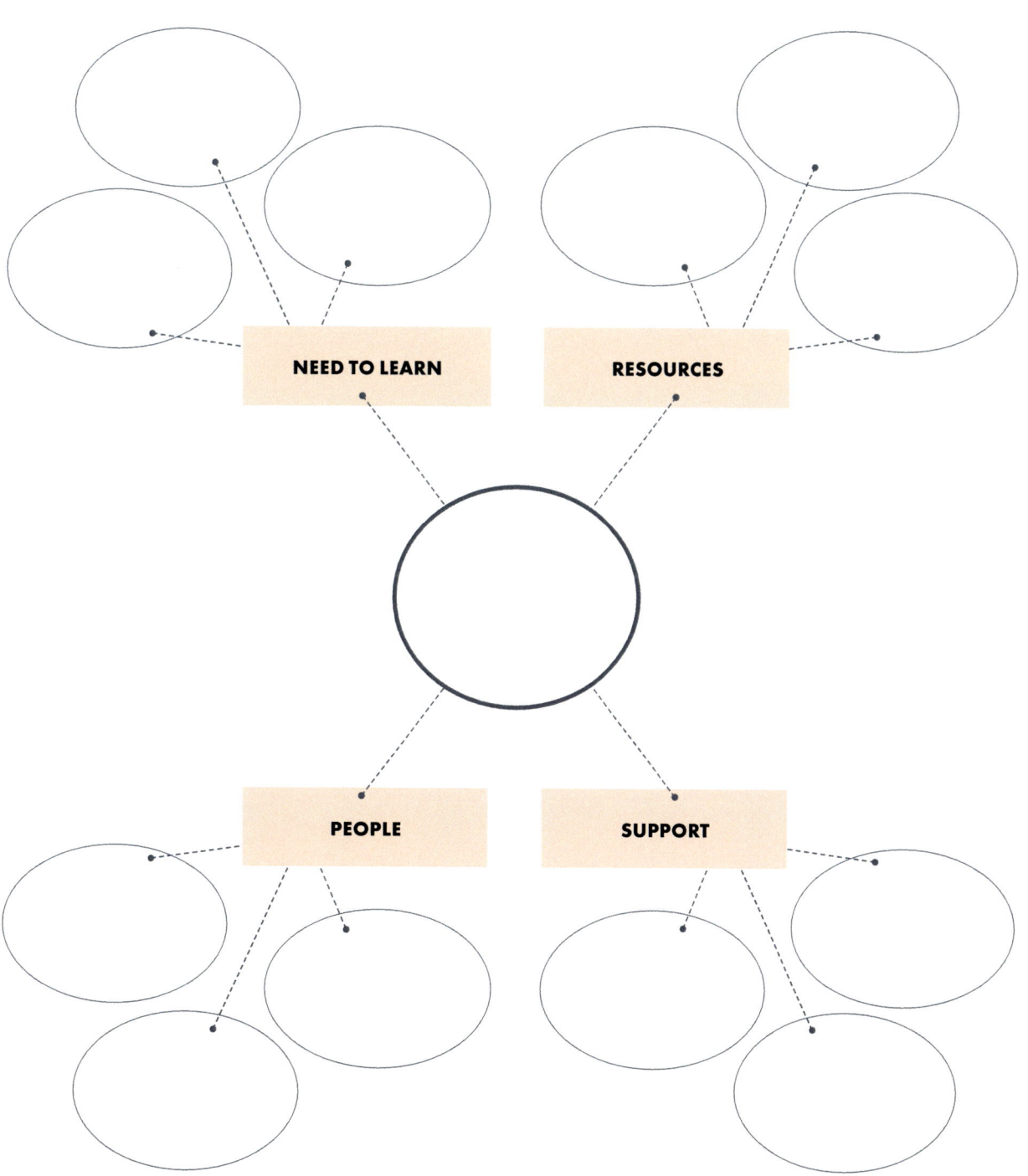

GOAL-PLANNING MAP

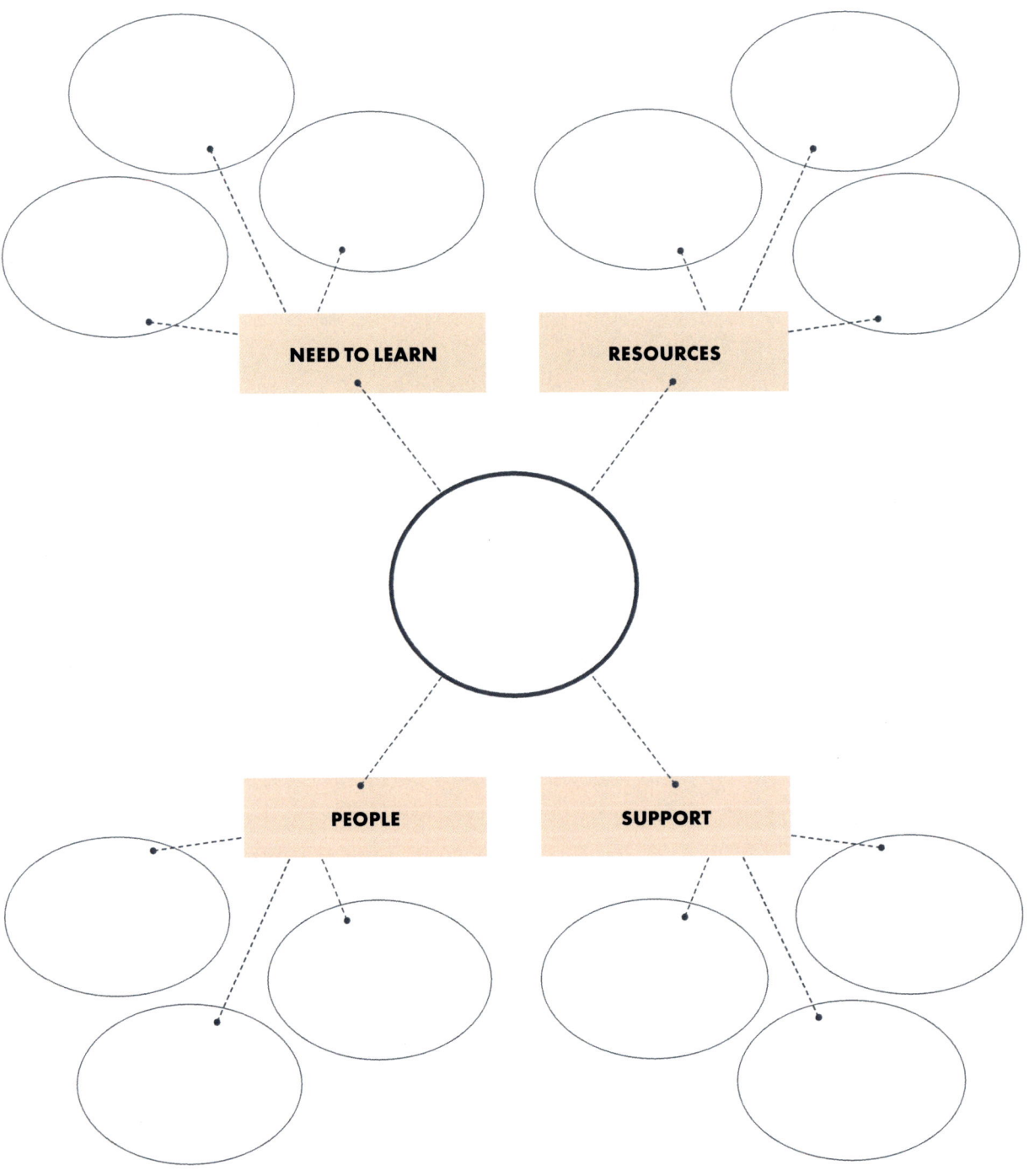

GOAL-PLANNING MAP

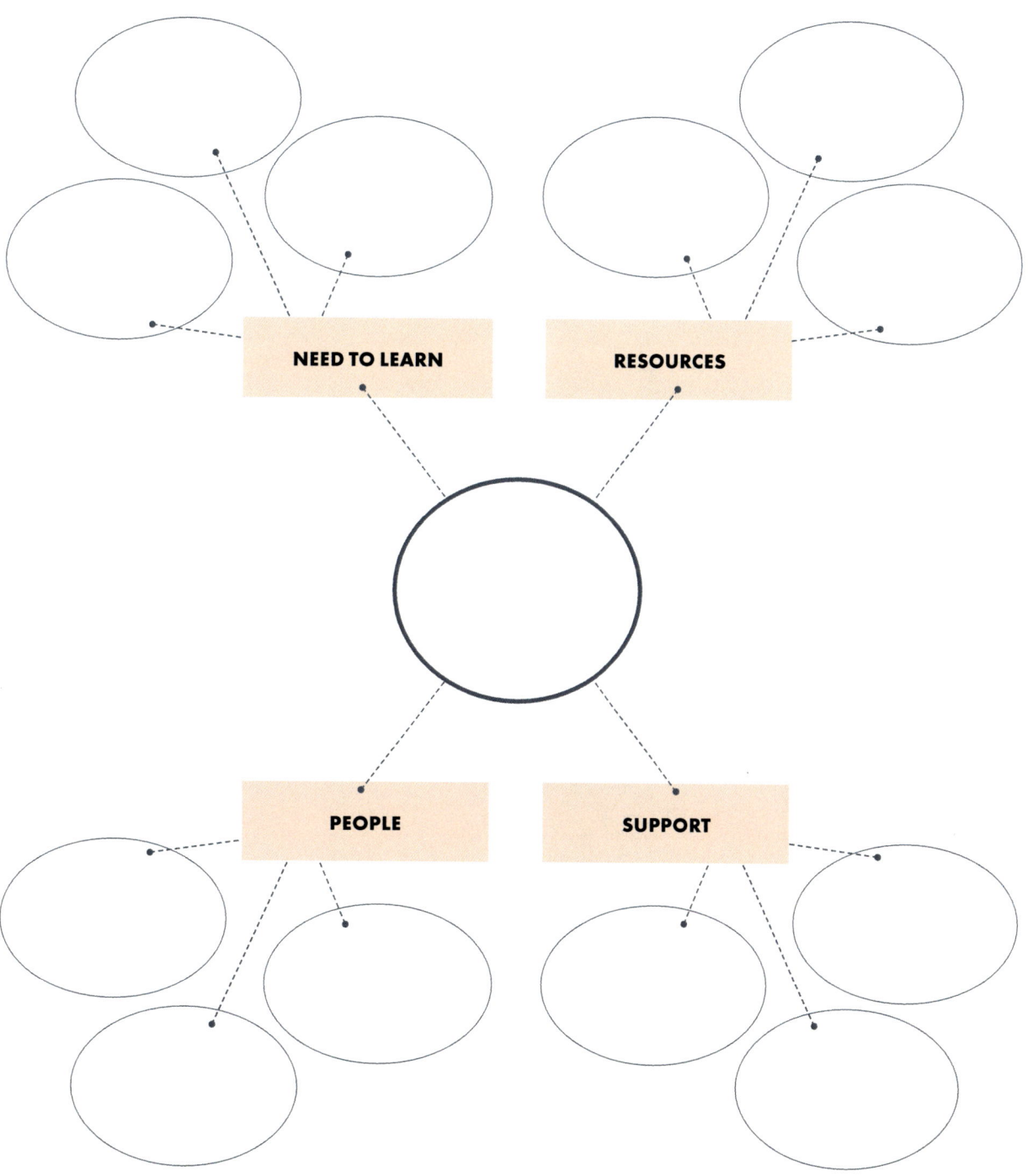

Finalize a *Plan* for Your Writing Life

Now that you've filled in your goal-planning maps, you're ready to summarize your writing plan. This is the last step before you plan the first quarter. It is a key step to establishing clarity and confidence in the direction you're taking.

As long as you keep your vision in mind and remind yourself of your why, you will be protected from the doubt and despair that threaten every writer in the midst of a project. You'll build solid habits and routines that keep you moving forward, on your way to creating a thriving, sustainable writing life.

Using the goals you've established, fill in the page titled "A Plan for My Writing Life," to summarize where you're headed this year. When you plan each quarter, referencing this page will help you stay on track and make revisions if you need to pivot. You've come a long way since we started this planning process. Well done for doing the hard work of laying a solid foundation!

A PLAN FOR MY WRITING LIFE

YEAR

My Vision Statement

This Year's Goals

1.

2.

3.

Why am I choosing these goals this year?

The Writer's Life
Quarterly Planning

Here we go! You've done the hard work of foundation building, creating your vision, sifting through the many ideas clamoring for your attention, and choosing the one, two, or three primary goal(s) to focus on as you move forward. Now you're wondering where to begin. That's where we're headed in planning the first quarter.

The quarterly planning process helps you select and prioritize your projects. We each come to our writing with a full life. Relationships, commitments, and responsibilities vie for our attention. In Psalm 90, we see Moses wrestling with the finite limitations of this earth life bounded by time. He ponders the meaning of life, trying to make sense of the brevity. Scholars believe this psalm was written during Moses's sojourn in the wilderness on the way to Canaan. If ever there were a suitable guide for perseverance, Moses is our man. In verse 12, he says,

> *Teach us to number our days, that we may gain a heart of wisdom.*

The Hebrew word here translated "number" means "to weigh out, to allot, to enumerate." What sage advice to heed as you learn how to plan your writing life using a quarterly approach. At the heart of this planning process, you are learning to weigh the options that compete for your time and to select priorities in line with your vision for your writing life.

Whatever this season brings, we're cheering you on. We want to see you set goals, implement a plan, and make adjustments as your writing journey emerges. We're focused on a steady transformation that develops your writing muscles as you find what works for your situation and your unique goals, cultivating a robust writing journey you can sustain over time.

We ask God to bless you with a steadfast spirit as you persevere in your writing life. May your determination be fueled by His strength, sufficient for the task at hand.

The First Quarter

January – February – March

It's time to identify your quarter plans for the next three months. Since you've set up a strong foundation, planning for each quarter, month, and week is easier to achieve with confidence.

As you select your focus for the first quarter, refer to the earlier page titled "A Plan for My Writing Life." Consider your plans for the next three months by answering this question: "What do I want to accomplish this quarter?" The goal that comes to mind will be your *key focus*.

Remember to pull out your "I Am a FlourishWriter" Scripture and affirmation to remind you why you started out on this journey. If you're feeling stuck or overwhelmed, refer to *The Writer's Block Remedy Kit* at the end of this planning guide.

What do I want to accomplish this quarter?

Select Goals and Action Steps for This Quarter

In light of your key focus for the quarter, brainstorm your goals and action steps. Use the space on the following page to note everything that comes to mind. Be sure to refer to your goal-planning maps. For example, a new writer wants to create a novel. This is her goal for the year. But she's a beginner. She doesn't know how to write a novel, so her starting place is to begin learning. Her quarter goal is to create a solid foundation to write her novel. Her action steps are (1) get a writing buddy, (2) purchase a course on writing a novel, and (3) learn to use Scrivener. She likely will not get the novel started and completed this year, but she will work consistently toward that goal.

As you brainstorm your action steps, these questions may be helpful:

- What do I need to know?
- What do I need to do?
- Are any actions dependent on other actions being completed first?
- Do I need to gather resources?
- What help do I need?

After you've brainstormed action steps, fill out your quarter plan. Write down your key focus for the quarter and your top one, two, or three goals, with accompanying action steps.

As you're working through this process, consider what you have going on for the next three months in your personal life. Doing so will give you realistic expectations about what you can accomplish in your writing life this quarter. Remember that most things take longer than you expect, especially when you're trying them for the first time.

Brainstorm Action Steps for This Quarter

FIRST QUARTER PLAN

JANUARY
FEBRUARY
MARCH

Key Focus

GOAL 1	GOAL 2	GOAL 3
Action Steps	Action Steps	Action Steps
○	○	○
○	○	○
○	○	○
○	○	○
○	○	○
○	○	○
○	○	○

January

Do you remember your first bicycle? I (Mindy) sure do. A yellow Schwinn named Daisy, with a banana seat, iridescent tassels sprouting from her handlebars, and a wicker basket on the front. She gave me a taste of independence as I sped down hills, jumped over moguls on the dirt path behind my house, and cycled to the ice-cream shop with money in my pocket.

Delicious freedom.

Sweet satisfaction.

Not all paths are downhill, however. My legs ached at climbing steep grades. When the ascent grew difficult, I'd rise off the seat, urging my full 70 pounds to pedal each rotation. Left. Right. Left. My muscles screamed, and I gasped for breath, but my determination held fast. I fixed my gaze on the crest.

How many strokes to the top, where gravity becomes my friend?

The steepest hill was my nemesis. It forced me to a standstill every time we met. I pumped hard nearly to the top, but as momentum waned, my balance gave out, and I jumped off the pedals. I hated walking the rest of the way. It tasted like failure. But Daisy and I didn't stop attempting the hill. I figured the more I met that mountain, the stronger I'd get.

I know I'm not the only one who was victorious over a childhood challenge.

What experience provided your first feelings of triumph?

Enjoy a moment to connect with your child's heart and revisit that sense of accomplishment. Remember how much effort it took? Remember, too, the exhilaration? You didn't give up. You kept your eyes on the goal, and no matter how many times you jumped off your bike and walked the rest of the way, each challenge brought you closer to eventual success.

Hold that memory close as you step out into your writing life this year. If you have a picture of yourself at that age, display it in your work area or place it here in *The Writer's Life Planning Guide*.

You're doing a new thing. As you build your writing muscles, stay connected to the tenacious child within.

Delicious freedom is fundamental to your identity in Christ.

Sweet satisfaction is your inheritance.

As you traverse the terrain of the writing life, enjoy the downhills, squealing with delight as the scenery rushes past in a colorful blur. Press up the mountains, reminded that every ascent makes you stronger. Although the difficult parts of the trail may be new to you, they're a natural part of the writing life, and we're cheering you to the top.

Together through this planning guide, we'll find the way and help you create the satisfying writing life you've been dreaming of. Let's get going.

My prayer for the month

January 2023

SUNDAY	MONDAY	TUESDAY	WEDNESDAY
1	2	3	4
8	9	10	11
15	16	17	18
22	23	24	25
29	30	31	

THURSDAY	FRIDAY	SATURDAY
5	6	7
12	13	14
19	20	21
26	27	28

Monthly Planning

Let's move from quarterly planning to gaining clarity and creating a solid monthly plan. You can focus on either one goal or several goals from the quarter plan during each month. Use the approach that works best for you.

As you plan, be aware that multitasking can be a drain on efficiency. On the one hand, too much variety in your focus for the month may cause distraction and overwhelm. You don't want to set unrealistic goals and create frustration. If it's a busy month, you may not be able to get the hours you need to make rapid progress, but you can stay consistent and work in the gaps to make steady progress nonetheless.

On the other hand, some variety can provide a nice break from larger tasks. You may find refreshment in breaking up an intense writing schedule with activities such as research, nurturing your community on social media, or meeting a colleague for coffee. Make sure you evaluate your family calendar. Do you need to plan around anything going on in your personal life? You'll be more motivated if you can stay consistent in your writing life, even if it's in small gaps throughout the month. Keep reminding yourself of your vision and your plan for the year. Pull out your "I Am a FlourishWriter" Scripture and affirmation and read them often.

When you complete your plan for a month, use the "Weekly Action Plan" pages or your personal planner to plan week by week.

PLAN FOR THE MONTH

January

Key Focus

Goals and Action Steps

1.

2.

3.

Weekly *Action* Plan

We've finally arrived at the beginning of implementation. You started with a vision for your writing life and moved to quarterly and monthly planning, and now the rubber meets the road in the weekly and daily plans. This is where we finally face the daily choices of how we spend our time.

Choose a day near the beginning of the week when you can spend a quiet 15–30 minutes reviewing the past week and planning the week ahead. Look at your family and work calendar then and review your plan for the month. Add your action items to the "Weekly Action Plan" pages or the personal planner you currently use.

Whatever you didn't get done last week can move forward. Don't berate yourself. Life happens. Plans must remain flexible to be useful. If this process starts to feel burdensome, you're going to avoid it. We naturally shy away from frustrating parts of life, so try your best to make this a positive experience.

Take the long view, and keep the goal in mind. Your big goals won't be accomplished in a day or two, a week or two, or even a month or two. Consistent progress—faithfully using the spaces of time you carve out each week—will add up over time. If all the wheels fall off your plan one week, just put them back on and move forward again the next week.

Moment by moment through each day, we hold onto a tenuous balance between responding to the day as it unfolds versus holding fast to a plan.

It's no mystery that self-discipline is needed. A big vision is inspiring, but daily action steps turn the vision into reality. Without daily action, a vision isn't anything more than a dream or a fantasy.

When planning, flexibility is a useful quality. Rigidity will cause stress. Above all, seek Holy Spirit guidance each moment of the day. Practice the dance between "my plan" and "God's plan." As much as possible, we want those plans to be synonymous, but holding fast with determination while letting go with submission requires walking by faith.

How do we follow through on our plans each day?

- Keep the vision and goals front and center.
- Revisit plans often.
- Listen for God's course correction.
- Connect to community, accountability, prayer support, and mentors.
- Find the grit to keep going, choosing a place to start back when we get off track.

Guard and walk out your vision by staying connected to God's Word. With Holy Spirit power and God's direction, you will begin to see your plan take shape.

WEEKLY ACTION PLAN

DATE: FROM _____ TO _____

- [ ] **SUNDAY**
- [ ] **MONDAY**
- [ ] **TUESDAY**
- [ ] **WEDNESDAY**
- [ ] **THURSDAY**
- [ ] **FRIDAY**
- [ ] **SATURDAY**

Weekly Focus

To-Dos

Notes

WEEKLY ACTION PLAN

DATE: FROM _____ TO _____

- [ ] **SUNDAY**
- [ ] **MONDAY**
- [ ] **TUESDAY**
- [ ] **WEDNESDAY**
- [ ] **THURSDAY**
- [ ] **FRIDAY**
- [ ] **SATURDAY**

Weekly Focus

To-Dos

Notes

WEEKLY ACTION PLAN

DATE: FROM _____ TO _____

- [ ] **SUNDAY**
- [ ] **MONDAY**
- [ ] **TUESDAY**
- [ ] **WEDNESDAY**
- [ ] **THURSDAY**
- [ ] **FRIDAY**
- [ ] **SATURDAY**

Weekly Focus

To-Dos

Notes

WEEKLY ACTION PLAN

DATE: FROM _____ TO _____

- [ ] **SUNDAY**
- [ ] **MONDAY**
- [ ] **TUESDAY**
- [ ] **WEDNESDAY**
- [ ] **THURSDAY**
- [ ] **FRIDAY**
- [ ] **SATURDAY**

Weekly Focus

To-Dos

- [ ]
- [ ]
- [ ]
- [ ]
- [ ]
- [ ]
- [ ]
- [ ]
- [ ]
- [ ]

Notes

WEEKLY ACTION PLAN

DATE: FROM _____ TO _____

- [ ] **SUNDAY**
- [ ] **MONDAY**
- [ ] **TUESDAY**
- [ ] **WEDNESDAY**
- [ ] **THURSDAY**
- [ ] **FRIDAY**
- [ ] **SATURDAY**

Weekly Focus

To-Dos

- ○
- ○
- ○
- ○
- ○
- ○
- ○
- ○
- ○
- ○

Notes

Month in Review

Use each "Month in Review" page to evaluate and reflect on the completed month before you plan for the next month. Conducting a review is essential to making adjustments in your plans. Many people fail to achieve their goals because they

- make plans but never look at them again;
- get frustrated when a plan doesn't work as anticipated;
- think "The plan's not working," rather than "What opportunities do I see?"; or
- feel like a failure when plans have to be adjusted.

We must observe each week and month as it emerges, holding the tension between the plan and reality, viewing challenges as growth opportunities rather than dead ends.

A growth mindset sees disruption through the lens of learning, energized by the chance to learn something new, to practice a new skill, and to grow as a person.

As you reflect, consider the following questions:

- What worked well?
- What didn't work well?
- What are you celebrating?
- What did you learn?
- What are you grateful for?
- Did you meet your goals?
- Do you need to adjust your goals for the next month?

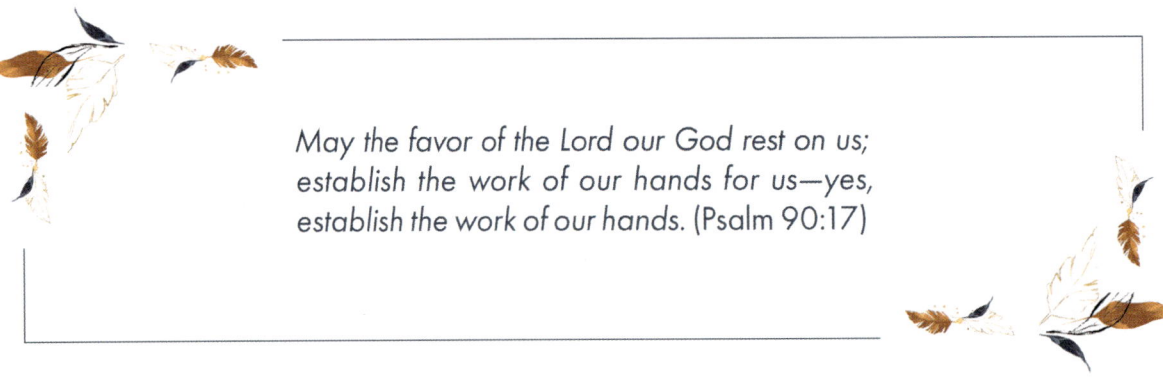

May the favor of the Lord our God rest on us; establish the work of our hands for us—yes, establish the work of our hands. (Psalm 90:17)

MONTH IN REVIEW

What worked well?

What didn't work well?

What am I celebrating?

What did I learn?

What am I grateful for?

Did I meet my goals? Do I need to adjust my goals for the next month?

February

When you decide to share your writing with others, you have no idea what's going to happen.

You write for days, weeks, months. You agonize and make sure everything is just right. Then you hesitantly click to publish, hold your breath, and . . . sometimes nothing much happens.

Sometimes no one notices. The gumption it took to put yourself out there seems to go unrewarded.

You want to be courageous and wear your "writer" name tag with confidence, to gather a community that delights in the message you're passionate about. How do you keep showing up when you see little response to content you spent hours crafting?

How do you keep writing words when you're not sure anyone is reading?

You seek satisfaction from a valid source. When we start writing our words for others, we have to guard our source of validation. It's tempting to work for "likes" and affirmation from others. Dopamine hits from those small wins train us to keep coming to "likes" for satisfaction.

But a writing life sustained over time calls for what we and Eugene Peterson refer to as "a long obedience in the same direction." We must keep showing up even when quick shots of dopamine are in short supply.

We seek to make peace with the perilous journey of the public writing life and to anchor ourselves to the satisfaction of writing sacred words. The only source of validation that will eternally satisfy is the daily bread we receive from time with Jesus.

You have chosen to step out in faith as you write the message on your heart. In the writing process, you will learn more about yourself and more about God.

What did you discover about your experience so far this year as you reviewed the month of January?

Nancy says, "Looking back on how the month went according to my goals, I saw that I had actually stayed on track . . . maybe because for once in my life, I had committed to a track in the first place. I'm encouraged to plan February since January went so well."

Melissa says, "I have struggled to engage with this process but refuse to step away from what I believe my heart is being stirred and drawn to. I have a strange roadblock currently. My first goal is to get on paper my quarterly goals by the end of February."

No matter how you're feeling about the planning process, prayerfully choose a starting place for this month. Review your "I Am a FlourishWriter" Scripture and affirmation as an encouragement for your heart. If you haven't yet, consider posting that page where you can read it every day. We pray that God blesses you with determination as you move into a new month.

My prayer for the month

February 2023

SUNDAY	MONDAY	TUESDAY	WEDNESDAY
			1
5	6	7	8
12	13	14	15
19	20	21	22
26	27	28	

THURSDAY	FRIDAY	SATURDAY
2	3	4
9	10	11
16	17	18
23	24	25

Notes for the Month

PLAN FOR THE MONTH

Key Focus

Goals and Action Steps

1.

2.

3.

WEEKLY ACTION PLAN

DATE: FROM _____ TO _____

- ☐ **SUNDAY**
- ☐ **MONDAY**
- ☐ **TUESDAY**
- ☐ **WEDNESDAY**
- ☐ **THURSDAY**
- ☐ **FRIDAY**
- ☐ **SATURDAY**

Weekly Focus

To-Dos

○
○
○
○
○
○
○
○
○
○
○

Notes

WEEKLY ACTION PLAN

DATE: FROM _____ TO _____

- [ ] **SUNDAY**
- [ ] **MONDAY**
- [ ] **TUESDAY**
- [ ] **WEDNESDAY**
- [ ] **THURSDAY**
- [ ] **FRIDAY**
- [ ] **SATURDAY**

Weekly Focus

To-Dos

- ○
- ○
- ○
- ○
- ○
- ○
- ○
- ○
- ○
- ○

Notes

WEEKLY ACTION PLAN

DATE: FROM _____ TO _____

- [ ] **SUNDAY**
- [ ] **MONDAY**
- [ ] **TUESDAY**
- [ ] **WEDNESDAY**
- [ ] **THURSDAY**
- [ ] **FRIDAY**
- [ ] **SATURDAY**

Weekly Focus

To-Dos

Notes

WEEKLY ACTION PLAN

DATE: FROM _____ TO _____

- [ ] **SUNDAY**
- [ ] **MONDAY**
- [ ] **TUESDAY**
- [ ] **WEDNESDAY**
- [ ] **THURSDAY**
- [ ] **FRIDAY**
- [ ] **SATURDAY**

Weekly Focus

To-Dos

Notes

WEEKLY ACTION PLAN

DATE: FROM _____ TO _____

- [ ] **SUNDAY**
- [ ] **MONDAY**
- [ ] **TUESDAY**
- [ ] **WEDNESDAY**
- [ ] **THURSDAY**
- [ ] **FRIDAY**
- [ ] **SATURDAY**

Weekly Focus

To-Dos

Notes

Notes

MONTH IN REVIEW

February

What worked well?

What didn't work well?

What am I celebrating?

What did I learn?

What am I grateful for?

Did I meet my goals? Do I need to adjust my goals for the next month?

> The great thing, if one can, is to stop regarding all the unpleasant things as interruptions of one's "own" or "real" life. The truth is of course that what one calls the interruptions are precisely one's real life—the life God is sending one day by day.
>
> *C. S. Lewis*

March

Remember when you decided to become more intentional in your writing life? What inspired you to take the plunge?

Cast your thoughts back to the first time you launched prayerfully into *The Writer's Life Planning Guide*. That first month rushed past. You blinked and now February too is complete.

As we step into March, the end of the first quarter is in the crosshairs. Yikes!

When you said yes to your writing life, you took a brave step to become more intentional. You had expectations about how it would play out.

Have the first 59 days surprised you?

We've heard from writers who say, "I've accomplished more than ever!" Others say, "Huh, it's slow going; the project is bigger than I thought."

Wherever you find yourself—elated or frustrated—remember the basic principle of *The Writer's Life Planning Guide*: goals translate to small daily actions. When you feel overwhelmed by a sizable goal and wonder if you are making progress, take a deep breath and choose one small task to work on today. Even 15 minutes can help you break out of deadlock.

When something becomes difficult, we tend to avoid it. The more we avoid, the harder it is to come back and engage. Is that a familiar pattern in your life? You don't want to do a task you know you need to do. You avoid it for weeks or months, then finally enough is enough. You do it . . . and it takes only 5 minutes! Isn't that the worst? The burden of an outstanding responsibility that weighed on your mind for weeks needed only a few minutes of attention.

As we head toward the end of our first quarter, Psalm 86:11 is our prayer over you.

> *Teach me your way, LORD, that I may rely on your faithfulness;*
> *give me an undivided heart, that I may fear your name.*

Speak that verse over yourself as a prayer. Sit with each word. *Teach. Faithfulness. Undivided.* That last word intrigued me (Mindy). Through an online interlinear search, I found a meaningful synonym: *united.*

My Scripture study led me to pray, "God, I ask you to unite my heart to you, to your calling, to your purposes in my writing life. I stand in holy awe at the place you've brought me. Help me rely on your faithfulness. I am your child. You are my Father. I trust in you to reveal the path one day at a time. Help me keep my goals in view, and show me the simple daily tasks I can do to move forward in my writing life this year."

We're cheering you on.

My prayer for the month

March 2023

SUNDAY	MONDAY	TUESDAY	WEDNESDAY
			1
5	6	7	8
12	13	14	15
19	20	21	22
26	27	28	29

THURSDAY	FRIDAY	SATURDAY
2	3	4
9	10	11
16	17	18
23	24	25
30	31	

Notes for the Month

PLAN FOR THE MONTH

Key Focus

Goals and Action Steps

1.

2.

3.

WEEKLY ACTION PLAN

DATE: FROM _____ TO _____

- [ ] **SUNDAY**
- [ ] **MONDAY**
- [ ] **TUESDAY**
- [ ] **WEDNESDAY**
- [ ] **THURSDAY**
- [ ] **FRIDAY**
- [ ] **SATURDAY**

Weekly Focus

To-Dos

- [ ]
- [ ]
- [ ]
- [ ]
- [ ]
- [ ]
- [ ]
- [ ]
- [ ]
- [ ]

Notes

WEEKLY ACTION PLAN

DATE: FROM _____ TO _____

- [ ] **SUNDAY**
- [ ] **MONDAY**
- [ ] **TUESDAY**
- [ ] **WEDNESDAY**
- [ ] **THURSDAY**
- [ ] **FRIDAY**
- [ ] **SATURDAY**

Weekly Focus

To-Dos

Notes

WEEKLY ACTION PLAN

DATE: FROM _____ TO _____

- [ ] **SUNDAY**
- [ ] **MONDAY**
- [ ] **TUESDAY**
- [ ] **WEDNESDAY**
- [ ] **THURSDAY**
- [ ] **FRIDAY**
- [ ] **SATURDAY**

Weekly Focus

To-Dos

Notes

WEEKLY ACTION PLAN

DATE: FROM _____ TO _____

- [ ] **SUNDAY**
- [ ] **MONDAY**
- [ ] **TUESDAY**
- [ ] **WEDNESDAY**
- [ ] **THURSDAY**
- [ ] **FRIDAY**
- [ ] **SATURDAY**

Weekly Focus

To-Dos

- [ ]
- [ ]
- [ ]
- [ ]
- [ ]
- [ ]
- [ ]
- [ ]
- [ ]
- [ ]

Notes

WEEKLY ACTION PLAN

DATE: FROM _____ TO _____

- ☐ **SUNDAY**
- ☐ **MONDAY**
- ☐ **TUESDAY**
- ☐ **WEDNESDAY**
- ☐ **THURSDAY**
- ☐ **FRIDAY**
- ☐ **SATURDAY**

Weekly Focus

To-Dos

Notes

Notes

MONTH IN REVIEW

What worked well?

What didn't work well?

What am I celebrating?

What did I learn?

What am I grateful for?

Did I meet my goals? Do I need to adjust my goals for the next month?

> Take seriously the story that God has given you to live. It's time to read your own life, because your story is the one that could set us all ablaze.
>
> *Dan B. Allender*

First Quarter in Review

January – February – March

Four times each year, you will review a quarter as a whole.

Refer to the page titled "A Plan for My Writing Life" and to the quarter plan you filled out at the beginning of this quarter.

Use the "First Quarter in Review" page to evaluate and reflect on the past quarter as you plan for the next.

Consider the following questions as you reflect:

- What worked well?
- What didn't work well?
- What are you celebrating?
- What did you learn?
- What are you grateful for?
- Did you meet your goals?
- Do you need to adjust your goals for the next quarter?

Make any adjustments you feel necessary to the plan for your writing life.

If you feel blocked or overwhelmed at any stage, stop and pray. Dig into *The Writer's Block Remedy Kit*. Its spiritual battle plan and soul-care remedies are designed for the times when overwhelm hits and hope wanes. We want you to find joy and peace in your writing life.

FIRST QUARTER IN REVIEW

JANUARY
FEBRUARY
MARCH

What worked well?

What didn't work well?

What am I celebrating?

What did I learn?

What am I grateful for?

Did I meet my goals? Do I need to adjust my goals for the next quarter?

The Writer's Life Second Quarter *Planning*

The *Second* Quarter

April – May – June

It's time to identify your quarter plans for the next three months. Since you've built a strong foundation, planning for each quarter, month, and week is easier to achieve with confidence.

As you select your focus for the second quarter, refer to the earlier page titled "A Plan for My Writing Life." Consider your plans for the next three months by answering this question: "What do I want to accomplish this quarter?" The goal that comes to mind will be your key focus.

Remember to pull out your "I Am a FlourishWriter" Scripture and affirmation to remind you why you started out on this journey. If you're feeling stuck or overwhelmed, refer to *The Writer's Block Remedy Kit* at the end of this planning guide.

What do I want to accomplish this quarter?

Select Goals and Action Steps for This Quarter

In light of your key focus for the quarter, brainstorm your goals and action steps. Use the space on the following page to note everything that comes to mind. Be sure to refer to your goal maps. Remember the new writer who wants to create a novel. This is her goal for the year. But she's a beginner. She is still learning how to write a novel. Her goal for the second quarter is to practice the planning exercises in the novel-writing course she's working through. Her action steps are (1) create a plot arc, (2) create a character arc for her protagonist, and (3) research any questions that arise from her planning. She likely will not get the novel started and completed this year, but she will work consistently toward that goal.

As you brainstorm your action steps, these questions may be helpful:

- What do I need to know?
- What do I need to do?
- Are any actions dependent on other actions being completed first?
- Do I need to gather resources?
- What help do I need?

After you've brainstormed action steps, fill out your quarter plan. Write down your key focus for the quarter and your top one, two, or three goals, with accompanying action steps.

As you're working through this process, consider what you have going on for the next three months in your personal life. Doing so will give you realistic expectations about what you can accomplish in your writing life this quarter. Remember that most things take longer than you expect, especially when you're trying them for the first time.

Brainstorm Action Steps

SECOND QUARTER PLAN

APRIL
MAY
JUNE

Key Focus

GOAL 1	GOAL 2	GOAL 3
Action Steps	Action Steps	Action Steps
○	○	○
○	○	○
○	○	○
○	○	○
○	○	○
○	○	○
○	○	○

April

The month of April ushers us into spring with fresh growth signaling new life. We pray you feel the warmth of sunshine and fragrance of open blossoms in your writing life as well. When you sit down with your plans, you may sense the sun slide behind the clouds. Often writers feel that they're not making enough progress.

Be on the lookout for a critical voice that may show up when you review your vision and goals. The spiritual battle plan in *The Writer's Block Remedy Kit* helps us identify the lies that attack us regarding our writing life. When we review our plans, we may face a fresh wave of limiting beliefs that arise. See if this thought sounds familiar:

> *I didn't make as much progress as I'd hoped. What made me think I was going to work consistently on my writing? I should've known it wouldn't come together like I planned. It's too much. It's too complicated. I don't have enough [fill in the blank].*

We all confront such thoughts. The voice of futility tempts us to despair. When you say yes to God and step out in obedience to write a message from the heart, the forces of evil kick up resistance. But we fight back with promises in the Word of God.

As we pray for you to find fresh clarity in the second quarter, we are reminded of a familiar portion of 1 Corinthians 13:12: *We see in a mirror, dimly* (NKJV); *We see things imperfectly, like puzzling reflections in a mirror* (NLT).

What does that Scripture have to do with our writing life? The Greek word translated "dimly" means "riddle" (*Strong's Concordance*), "a question or statement intentionally phrased to require ingenuity in ascertaining its answer or meaning, typically presented as a game" (*Oxford Reference*).

What if we see our planning as a game requiring ingenuity, with God as our coach? Doesn't that take the pressure off? At FlourishWriters, we're serious planners, but we recognize our limitations. We research, observe, and pray, aware that we see things imperfectly. Nevertheless, we choose goals and go for it wholeheartedly.

Each step is a grand experiment.

Even if a project doesn't turn out quite like we thought, everything we try adds to our experience, which builds out our writer's toolbox. We gather data and learn. If we allow ourselves to become paralyzed by fear of failure, we don't act. If we wait for perfect clarity to move forward, we become stuck.

As we complete the first quarter and head into the second, we encourage you to think of your writing life as a game, a riddle that requires ingenuity to solve. Games are fun, lighthearted, and exciting. When you take a learning approach, you gather information, pray, and then take the next step.

If you feel puzzled—if you see the situation dimly—take heart. Someday you'll see with complete clarity, but for now, you're doing the best you can and obeying as best you know how. God is the only one with perfect vision. If you're feeling uncertain, that doesn't disqualify you—it makes you human.

As you plan for the second quarter, start with your "I Am a FlourishWriter" Scripture and affirmation. Ask the Lord to keep your thoughts positive and connected with the Spirit-breathed vision for your writing life.

Don't get bogged down in the planning process. Remember to check back in with the planning you did at the beginning of the year, so you can see where you are and choose where to go next. If you need to make a course correction, do it. No shame. No regrets. Just forward progress.

Here's to flourishing in your writing life, one step at a time.

My prayer for the month

April 2023

SUNDAY	MONDAY	TUESDAY	WEDNESDAY
2	3	4	5
9	10	11	12
16	17	18	19
23 / 30	24	25	26

THURSDAY	FRIDAY	SATURDAY
		1
6	7	8
13	14	15
20	21	22
27	28	29

Notes for the Month

PLAN FOR THE MONTH

Key Focus

Goals and Action Steps

1.

2.

3.

WEEKLY ACTION PLAN

DATE: FROM _____ TO _____

- [ ] **SUNDAY**
- [ ] **MONDAY**
- [ ] **TUESDAY**
- [ ] **WEDNESDAY**
- [ ] **THURSDAY**
- [ ] **FRIDAY**
- [ ] **SATURDAY**

Weekly Focus

To-Dos

Notes

WEEKLY ACTION PLAN

DATE: FROM _____ TO _____

- [ ] **SUNDAY**
- [ ] **MONDAY**
- [ ] **TUESDAY**
- [ ] **WEDNESDAY**
- [ ] **THURSDAY**
- [ ] **FRIDAY**
- [ ] **SATURDAY**

Weekly Focus

To-Dos

- [ ]
- [ ]
- [ ]
- [ ]
- [ ]
- [ ]
- [ ]
- [ ]
- [ ]
- [ ]

Notes

WEEKLY ACTION PLAN

DATE: FROM _____ TO _____

- [ ] **SUNDAY**
- [ ] **MONDAY**
- [ ] **TUESDAY**
- [ ] **WEDNESDAY**
- [ ] **THURSDAY**
- [ ] **FRIDAY**
- [ ] **SATURDAY**

Weekly Focus

To-Dos

Notes

WEEKLY ACTION PLAN

DATE: FROM _____ TO _____

- [ ] **SUNDAY**
- [ ] **MONDAY**
- [ ] **TUESDAY**
- [ ] **WEDNESDAY**
- [ ] **THURSDAY**
- [ ] **FRIDAY**
- [ ] **SATURDAY**

Weekly Focus

To-Dos

- [ ]
- [ ]
- [ ]
- [ ]
- [ ]
- [ ]
- [ ]
- [ ]
- [ ]
- [ ]

Notes

WEEKLY ACTION PLAN

DATE: FROM _____ TO _____

- [ ] **SUNDAY**
- [ ] **MONDAY**
- [ ] **TUESDAY**
- [ ] **WEDNESDAY**
- [ ] **THURSDAY**
- [ ] **FRIDAY**
- [ ] **SATURDAY**

Weekly Focus

To-Dos

- [ ]
- [ ]
- [ ]
- [ ]
- [ ]
- [ ]
- [ ]
- [ ]
- [ ]
- [ ]
- [ ]

Notes

Notes

MONTH IN REVIEW

April

What worked well?

What didn't work well?

What am I celebrating?

What did I learn?

What am I grateful for?

Did I meet my goals? Do I need to adjust my goals for the next month?

> *Celebrate progress, not perfection.
> Little-by-little progress is still progress.*
>
> — *Lara Casey*

May

May is a beautiful month the world over. Those in the northern hemisphere are full into spring, with trees leafing out and flowers on display. Our southern hemisphere neighbors bask in the cool breezes of autumn as harvest colors transform the landscape.

What does this month hold for your writing life? You might be anxious and asking, "Have I made enough progress?"

Consider one of our slogans at FlourishWriters: "You're not behind! Jump in where you are."

Our author friend Allen Arnold encourages us to take the road less traveled in our writing life. He urges us to focus not on the end goal but on the journey. His definition of success is simple. Success is co-creating with God. *That's it.*

God cares more about who we are becoming than what we accomplish. *Who we are is more important than what we write.* Let those words sink in.

When we're sprinting for the finish line rather than enjoying the journey, we have a tendency to grasp for formula. We think, *Teach me the tricks. Tell me how to get this project out. Quickly, let's get moving.*

We long to write a bestseller, to figure out the secret formula the professionals know. Instead, let's take a deep breath and s.l.o.w. d.o.w.n. Get on God's timetable. Create space for your message to be birthed in due season on a God-ordained timeline. Just as a due date in pregnancy is a best guess, so the full term of a writing project is more mystery than prescriptive schedule. With all the technology at our disposal, writing from the heart is still an organic, biological process. Only God knows the timing.

Formulas create formulaic messages. Creating with God births Spirit-breathed messages. Which do you want?

We remind our writer heart to let God be the source of our validation. When we slow down and listen, we create what we were born to create. You have personal power and authority to speak to the issues God has overcome in your life. When you stand in the power of a surrendered heart, your story ignites freedom and demolishes strongholds. That's why no one else can share your message. That's why your message threatens the forces of evil.

Your words are filled with authority. Your purpose is far greater than merely sharing a message. God's majesty revealed in your story opens a portal between heaven and earth. Your words invite the kingdom of God to be revealed on earth as it is in heaven.

Crafting this kind of message follows no formula, and it's worth the wait. As Paul says, *By no means do I count myself an expert in all of this, but I've got my eye on the goal, where God is beckoning us onward—to Jesus. I'm off and running, and I'm not turning back. So let's keep focused on that goal, those of us who want everything God has for us* (Philippians 3:14–15 MSG).

We're here with you, keeping our eyes on Jesus.

My prayer for the month

May 2023

SUNDAY	MONDAY	TUESDAY	WEDNESDAY
	1	2	3
7	8	9	10
14	15	16	17
21	22	23	24
28	29	30	31

THURSDAY	FRIDAY	SATURDAY
4	5	6
11	12	13
18	19	20
25	26	27

Notes for the Month

PLAN FOR THE MONTH

Key Focus

Goals and Action Steps

1.

2.

3.

WEEKLY ACTION PLAN

DATE: FROM _____ TO _____

- [ ] **SUNDAY**
- [ ] **MONDAY**
- [ ] **TUESDAY**
- [ ] **WEDNESDAY**
- [ ] **THURSDAY**
- [ ] **FRIDAY**
- [ ] **SATURDAY**

Weekly Focus

To-Dos

Notes

WEEKLY ACTION PLAN

DATE: FROM _____ TO _____

- [ ] **SUNDAY**
- [ ] **MONDAY**
- [ ] **TUESDAY**
- [ ] **WEDNESDAY**
- [ ] **THURSDAY**
- [ ] **FRIDAY**
- [ ] **SATURDAY**

Weekly Focus

To-Dos

- [ ]
- [ ]
- [ ]
- [ ]
- [ ]
- [ ]
- [ ]
- [ ]
- [ ]
- [ ]

Notes

WEEKLY ACTION PLAN

DATE: FROM _____ TO _____

- [ ] **SUNDAY**
- [ ] **MONDAY**
- [ ] **TUESDAY**
- [ ] **WEDNESDAY**
- [ ] **THURSDAY**
- [ ] **FRIDAY**
- [ ] **SATURDAY**

Weekly Focus

To-Dos

- ○
- ○
- ○
- ○
- ○
- ○
- ○
- ○
- ○
- ○

Notes

WEEKLY ACTION PLAN

DATE: FROM _____ TO _____

- [ ] **SUNDAY**
- [ ] **MONDAY**
- [ ] **TUESDAY**
- [ ] **WEDNESDAY**
- [ ] **THURSDAY**
- [ ] **FRIDAY**
- [ ] **SATURDAY**

Weekly Focus

To-Dos

Notes

WEEKLY ACTION PLAN

DATE: FROM _____ TO _____

☐ **SUNDAY**

☐ **MONDAY**

☐ **TUESDAY**

☐ **WEDNESDAY**

☐ **THURSDAY**

☐ **FRIDAY**

☐ **SATURDAY**

Weekly Focus

To-Dos

○
○
○
○
○
○
○
○
○
○
○

Notes

Notes

MONTH IN REVIEW

May

What worked well?

What didn't work well?

What am I celebrating?

What did I learn?

What am I grateful for?

Did I meet my goals? Do I need to adjust my goals for the next month?

> *I've long since stopped feeling guilty about taking being time; it's something we all need for our spiritual health, and often we don't take enough of it.*
>
> — *Madeleine L'Engle*

June

Here comes summer! As we prepare for a change in routine, we desire to prepare our hearts and minds to meet the new season.

We refer to this time of year as the "messy middle," as we confront shifting schedules and new expectations. We always *pause, ponder, and prepare* when we begin a new month, especially when it's a new season.

As we begin this final month of the second quarter, we're jumping into summer. How does that look practically?

Give yourself grace to adjust your writing plans to accommodate this new season.

Allow yourself more time during the first week of this month to adjust for changes on the horizon.

Look ahead into the third quarter, and begin planning or preparing summer plans for family time, vacations, or special projects.

We want to help you prepare your heart for a new season. We desire to see the power of God come alive in your life each day, for you to soak up all the goodness this season offers. Every season has special gifts from God.

Kari says, "When I started my blog last fall, I added a new post every week. Since Christmas it has been a constant struggle. I published my fifth post for the year yesterday, and it was exactly what was needed for a friend who lost her husband earlier this year. I'm so encouraged that God would use my writing to meet her where she is, at just the time she needed it. That encourages me to press on!"

Nancy says, "I am encouraged by fellow bloggers who reached out to me this week, one asking to share guest blogs, one asking me to proof her work. The network God is creating through FlourishWriters is such a blessing."

Marie says, "I love the analogy of stones marking God at work—in me and through me. This past month has not been as productive in my writing life, so I feel like my stone says 'failure'—but looking back over the past six months reveals God has helped me gather a pile of stones."

Carolyn says, "I struggle a lot in looking backwards, but as I think about my last five months, I am surprised. I actually have my devotion almost ready to send for feedback, and then it is book cover and interior design I need to focus on. I keep hearing this voice telling me no one knows who I am and so I won't sell anything. It is true, I do live a quiet existence, but God's got the marketing plans. I will trust Him with them."

What does the Lord have in store for you? What can you trust Him with?

As always, we are praying for you.

My prayer for the month

June 2023

SUNDAY	MONDAY	TUESDAY	WEDNESDAY
4	5	6	7
11	12	13	14
18	19	20	21
25	26	27	28

THURSDAY	FRIDAY	SATURDAY
1	2	3
8	9	10
15	16	17
22	23	24
29	30	

Notes for the Month

PLAN FOR THE MONTH

Key Focus

Goals and Action Steps

1.

2.

3.

WEEKLY ACTION PLAN

DATE: FROM _____ TO _____

☐ **SUNDAY**

☐ **MONDAY**

☐ **TUESDAY**

☐ **WEDNESDAY**

☐ **THURSDAY**

☐ **FRIDAY**

☐ **SATURDAY**

Weekly Focus

To-Dos

Notes

WEEKLY ACTION PLAN

DATE: FROM _____ TO _____

- [ ] **SUNDAY**
- [ ] **MONDAY**
- [ ] **TUESDAY**
- [ ] **WEDNESDAY**
- [ ] **THURSDAY**
- [ ] **FRIDAY**
- [ ] **SATURDAY**

Weekly Focus

To-Dos

- [ ]
- [ ]
- [ ]
- [ ]
- [ ]
- [ ]
- [ ]
- [ ]
- [ ]
- [ ]

Notes

THE WRITER'S LIFE PLANNING GUIDE

WEEKLY ACTION PLAN

DATE: FROM _____ TO _____

- [ ] **SUNDAY**
- [ ] **MONDAY**
- [ ] **TUESDAY**
- [ ] **WEDNESDAY**
- [ ] **THURSDAY**
- [ ] **FRIDAY**
- [ ] **SATURDAY**

Weekly Focus

To-Dos

Notes

WEEKLY ACTION PLAN

DATE: FROM _____ TO _____

- [ ] **SUNDAY**
- [ ] **MONDAY**
- [ ] **TUESDAY**
- [ ] **WEDNESDAY**
- [ ] **THURSDAY**
- [ ] **FRIDAY**
- [ ] **SATURDAY**

Weekly Focus

To-Dos

- [ ]
- [ ]
- [ ]
- [ ]
- [ ]
- [ ]
- [ ]
- [ ]
- [ ]
- [ ]

Notes

WEEKLY ACTION PLAN

DATE: FROM _____ TO _____

- ☐ **SUNDAY**
- ☐ **MONDAY**
- ☐ **TUESDAY**
- ☐ **WEDNESDAY**
- ☐ **THURSDAY**
- ☐ **FRIDAY**
- ☐ **SATURDAY**

Weekly Focus

To-Dos

○
○
○
○
○
○
○
○
○
○

Notes

Notes

MONTH IN REVIEW

What worked well?

What didn't work well?

What am I celebrating?

What did I learn?

What am I grateful for?

Did I meet my goals? Do I need to adjust my goals for the next month?

> "All this," David said, "I have in writing as a result of the LORD's hand on me, and he enabled me to understand all the details of the plan."
>
> *1 Chronicles 28:19*

Second Quarter in Review

April – May – June

It's time to review the second quarter as a whole.

Refer to the page titled "A Plan for My Writing Life" and to the quarter plan you filled out at the beginning of this quarter.

Use the "Second Quarter in Review" page to evaluate and reflect on the past quarter as you plan for the next.

Consider the following questions as you reflect:

- What worked well?
- What didn't work well?
- What are you celebrating?
- What did you learn?
- What are you grateful for?
- Did you meet your goals?
- Do you need to adjust your goals for the next quarter?

Make any adjustments you feel necessary to the plan for your writing life.

If you feel blocked or overwhelmed at any stage, stop and pray. Dig into *The Writer's Block Remedy Kit*. Its spiritual battle plan and soul-care remedies are designed for times when overwhelm hits and hope wanes. We want you to find joy and peace in your writing life.

SECOND QUARTER IN REVIEW

APRIL
MAY
JUNE

What worked well?

What didn't work well?

What am I celebrating?

What did I learn?

What am I grateful for?

Did I meet my goals? Do I need to adjust my goals for the next quarter?

The Writer's Life
Third Quarter *Planning*

The *Third* Quarter

July – August – September

It's time to identify your quarter plans for the next three months. Since you've built a strong foundation, planning for each quarter, month, and week is easier to achieve with confidence.

As you select your focus for the third quarter, refer to the page titled "A Plan for My Writing Life." Consider your plans for the next three months by answering this question: "What do I want to accomplish this quarter?" The goal that comes to mind will be your key focus.

Remember to pull out your "I Am a FlourishWriter" Scripture and affirmation to remind you why you started out on this journey. If you're feeling stuck or overwhelmed, refer to *The Writer's Block Remedy Kit* at the end of this planning guide.

What do I want to accomplish this quarter?

Select Goals and Action Steps for This Quarter

In light of your key focus for the quarter, brainstorm your goals and action steps. Use the space on the following page to note everything that comes to mind. Be sure to refer to your goal-planning maps. Remember the new writer who wants to create a novel. This is her goal for the year. But she is still learning how to write a novel. Her goal for the third quarter is to flesh out the character sketches for her novel. Her action steps are (1) journal in the voice of each main character, (2) identify the Enneagram type of each character, and (3) practice writing scenes where the main characters interact. She likely will not get the novel started and completed this year, but she will work consistently toward that goal.

As you brainstorm your action steps, these questions may be helpful:

- What do I need to know?
- What do I need to do?
- Are any actions dependent on other actions being completed first?
- Do I need to gather resources?
- What help do I need?

After you've brainstormed action steps, fill out your quarter plan. Write down your key focus for the quarter and your top one, two, or three goals, with accompanying action steps.

As you're working through this process, consider what you have going on for the next three months in your personal life. Doing so will give you realistic expectations about what you can accomplish in your writing life this quarter.

Brainstorm Action Steps

THIRD QUARTER PLAN

JULY
AUGUST
SEPTEMBER

Key Focus

GOAL 1	GOAL 2	GOAL 3
Action Steps	Action Steps	Action Steps
○	○	○
○	○	○
○	○	○
○	○	○
○	○	○
○	○	○
○	○	○

July

We've had Psalm 27 on our hearts as we launch into the third quarter. When I (Mindy) looked up verse 13, it surprised me how variable the translations are.

> *I remain confident of this: I will see the goodness of the LORD in the land of the living.* (NIV)

> *I believe that I shall look upon the goodness of the LORD in the land of the living!* (ESV)

> *I would have lost heart unless I had believed that I would see the goodness of the LORD In the land of the living.* (NKJV)

> *I would have despaired had I not believed that I would see the goodness of the LORD In the land of the living.* (AMP)

Remain confident . . . believe . . . lost heart . . . despaired . . . My writerly sensibilities notice that some words stir me more than others. The version I like best calls out *losing heart*. This connects with my experience more than *remaining confident*.

The NIV version doesn't capture any of the "unless I had believed" message. What an omission! Without belief we don't have confidence, but how do I believe when I'm facing despair and losing heart?

Charles Spurgeon says, "The words in this verse at which I catch are these, 'Unless I had believed to see.' Most people see to believe, but in David's case the process was reversed, and put into gospel order: he believed to see."

Reading these different translations side by side provides an example of how to choose words thoughtfully when we share the message on our heart. May Holy Spirit inspire the translation of your message into words on the page.

May Holy Spirit also inspire your reflection on the first half of this year and your planning for the second half. Use this time to press into God and receive His fresh manna for right now.

Your goals may need to shift in response to what happened during the first half of this year. Let them change. Adjusting plans is not a failure. It's simply responding with acceptance to what is, yielding to the reality of how the year is rolling out.

Teresa says, "I'm learning 'not writing' times are also important. My brain needs down time. Sometimes the stewpot needs to just simmer."

Receive our prayer over you, from Psalm 27:13–14 in The Passion Translation:

> *Yet I believe with all my heart that I will see again your goodness, Yahweh, in the land of life eternal! Here's what I've learned through it all:*
>
> *Don't give up; don't be impatient;*
>
> *be entwined as one with the Lord.*
>
> *Be brave and courageous, and never lose hope.*
>
> *Yes, keep on waiting—for he will never disappoint you!*

My prayer for the month

July 2023

SUNDAY	MONDAY	TUESDAY	WEDNESDAY
2	3	4	5
9	10	11	12
16	17	18	19
23 / 30	24 / 31	25	26

THURSDAY	FRIDAY	SATURDAY
		1
6	7	8
13	14	15
20	21	22
27	28	29

Notes for the Month

PLAN FOR THE MONTH

Key Focus

Goals and Action Steps

1.

2.

3.

WEEKLY ACTION PLAN

DATE: FROM _____ TO _____

- [ ] **SUNDAY**
- [ ] **MONDAY**
- [ ] **TUESDAY**
- [ ] **WEDNESDAY**
- [ ] **THURSDAY**
- [ ] **FRIDAY**
- [ ] **SATURDAY**

Weekly Focus

To-Dos

Notes

WEEKLY ACTION PLAN

DATE: FROM _____ TO _____

- ☐ **SUNDAY**
- ☐ **MONDAY**
- ☐ **TUESDAY**
- ☐ **WEDNESDAY**
- ☐ **THURSDAY**
- ☐ **FRIDAY**
- ☐ **SATURDAY**

Weekly Focus

To-Dos

○
○
○
○
○
○
○
○
○
○

Notes

WEEKLY ACTION PLAN

DATE: FROM _____ TO _____

☐ **SUNDAY**

☐ **MONDAY**

☐ **TUESDAY**

☐ **WEDNESDAY**

☐ **THURSDAY**

☐ **FRIDAY**

☐ **SATURDAY**

Weekly Focus

To-Dos

Notes

WEEKLY ACTION PLAN

DATE: FROM _____ TO _____

- [ ] **SUNDAY**
- [ ] **MONDAY**
- [ ] **TUESDAY**
- [ ] **WEDNESDAY**
- [ ] **THURSDAY**
- [ ] **FRIDAY**
- [ ] **SATURDAY**

Weekly Focus

To-Dos

Notes

WEEKLY ACTION PLAN

DATE: FROM _____ TO _____

- [ ] **SUNDAY**
- [ ] **MONDAY**
- [ ] **TUESDAY**
- [ ] **WEDNESDAY**
- [ ] **THURSDAY**
- [ ] **FRIDAY**
- [ ] **SATURDAY**

Weekly Focus

To-Dos

- ○
- ○
- ○
- ○
- ○
- ○
- ○
- ○
- ○
- ○

Notes

Notes

MONTH IN REVIEW

What worked well?

What didn't work well?

What am I celebrating?

What did I learn?

What am I grateful for?

Did I meet my goals? Do I need to adjust my goals for the next month?

> *Knowing what to focus on now, and what to hold off until later, can mean the difference between success and burn out.*
>
> — *Todd Herman*

August

The month of August is placed precariously in an exhausting stretch, where the energy of New Year's resolutions is long gone, while summer diversions wage war against your schedule. The diversions may be welcome—like kids or grands home for the summer, camps, and vacations—but they still compete for your writing time.

Shannon posted in the private community space, "I'm so behind. I thought I would be able to make time, but with two kids home with me all the time, moving into a new house, and now a two-week vacation next month, maybe I was being too ambitious? I really wanted to make this work, but it may not be the right season."

Nipping at the heels of a demanding summer schedule is the fall season, when life gets really crazy. You feel the stress creeping up your shoulders, lodging in your neck. We know the feeling from experience.

How do you deal with unmet expectations and wait for life to settle down so you can get to your projects?

Instead of waiting, consider that in the chaos, in the craziness, is where creativity happens. That thought is counterintuitive. But if you're waiting for the perfect space of time to write, you'll never find it. If you allow yourself to get fed up and quit, then you're really done for. But you won't do that, will you?

Making writing a priority means making hard choices. When you say yes to writing, you have to say no to other demands on your time. Jerry Jenkins, author of over 200 books, tells it this way:

"If you wait until you *find* the time to write, you may never start. When I was working a full-time job and helping my wife raise our sons, I couldn't *find* the time to write either. . . . I had to *make* the time.

"After my family went to bed, I placed two kitchen chairs in front of the couch with a plank of plywood spanning them. I set my typewriter atop it and wrote till midnight every night. It wasn't convenient. It wasn't glamorous. But I made it work.

"The question wasn't: *Do I have time to write?* It was: *How badly do I want to be an author?* If you're serious about your writing dreams, stop trying to *find* the time and instead *make* the time to write.

"Dreamers talk about writing. Writers write."

OK, Jerry, thanks for the straight talk.

As you review July and plan for August, prayerfully consider what God has for you in the next four weeks. Is it a time of rest and recreation before children return to school? Is it a time to block off morning or evening hours as you determine to make progress on your writing project? Make your plans and guard your decisions.

My prayer for the month

August 2023

SUNDAY	MONDAY	TUESDAY	WEDNESDAY
		1	2
6	7	8	9
13	14	15	16
20	21	22	23
27	28	29	30

THURSDAY	FRIDAY	SATURDAY
3	4	5
10	11	12
17	18	19
24	25	26
31		

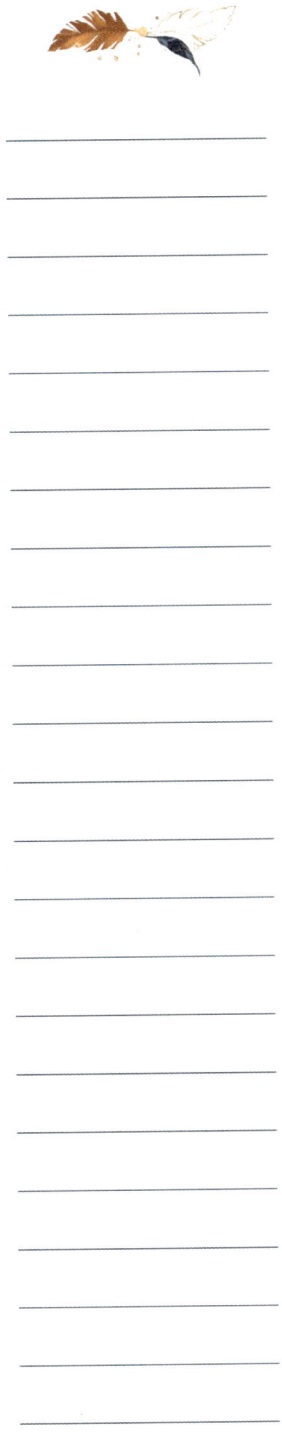

Notes for the Month

PLAN FOR THE MONTH

August

Key Focus

Goals and Action Steps

1.

2.

3.

WEEKLY ACTION PLAN

DATE: FROM _____ TO _____

- [ ] **SUNDAY**
- [ ] **MONDAY**
- [ ] **TUESDAY**
- [ ] **WEDNESDAY**
- [ ] **THURSDAY**
- [ ] **FRIDAY**
- [ ] **SATURDAY**

Weekly Focus

To-Dos

- [ ]
- [ ]
- [ ]
- [ ]
- [ ]
- [ ]
- [ ]
- [ ]
- [ ]
- [ ]

Notes

WEEKLY ACTION PLAN

DATE: FROM _____ TO _____

- [ ] **SUNDAY**
- [ ] **MONDAY**
- [ ] **TUESDAY**
- [ ] **WEDNESDAY**
- [ ] **THURSDAY**
- [ ] **FRIDAY**
- [ ] **SATURDAY**

Weekly Focus

_____
_____
_____
_____
_____

To-Dos

- ○ _____
- ○ _____
- ○ _____
- ○ _____
- ○ _____
- ○ _____
- ○ _____
- ○ _____
- ○ _____
- ○ _____

Notes

WEEKLY ACTION PLAN

DATE: FROM _____ TO _____

☐ **SUNDAY**

☐ **MONDAY**

☐ **TUESDAY**

☐ **WEDNESDAY**

☐ **THURSDAY**

☐ **FRIDAY**

☐ **SATURDAY**

Weekly Focus

To-Dos

○
○
○
○
○
○
○
○
○

Notes

WEEKLY ACTION PLAN

DATE: FROM _____ TO _____

- [ ] **SUNDAY**
- [ ] **MONDAY**
- [ ] **TUESDAY**
- [ ] **WEDNESDAY**
- [ ] **THURSDAY**
- [ ] **FRIDAY**
- [ ] **SATURDAY**

Weekly Focus

To-Dos

Notes

WEEKLY ACTION PLAN

DATE: FROM _____ TO _____

- [ ] **SUNDAY**
- [ ] **MONDAY**
- [ ] **TUESDAY**
- [ ] **WEDNESDAY**
- [ ] **THURSDAY**
- [ ] **FRIDAY**
- [ ] **SATURDAY**

Weekly Focus

To-Dos

Notes

Notes

MONTH IN REVIEW

What worked well?

What didn't work well?

What am I celebrating?

What did I learn?

What am I grateful for?

Did I meet my goals? Do I need to adjust my goals for the next month?

> *Our humanity comes to its fullest bloom in giving. We become beautiful people when we give whatever we can give: a smile, a handshake, a kiss, an embrace, a word of love, a present, a part of our life … all of our life.*
>
> — *Henri J. M. Nouwen*

September

Remember when you were a tot and Christmas took f-o-r-e-v-e-r to arrive? Now you're all grown up. Your days and weeks rush past. Your schedule has become a bucking bronco. You're holding on for dear life.

But you have *The Writer's Life Planning Guide*. And it's only September. You're just two-thirds of the way through the calendar year. Four glorious months stretch before you, full of potential.

We encourage you to reconnect with the vision that launched you into this writing journey months ago. It may have gotten buried under the busyness of life, but Psalm 40 invites us to let God pull us out of the ditch and place our feet on solid rock.

> *I waited and waited and waited for God.*
>   *At last he looked; finally he listened.*
> *He lifted me out of the ditch,*
>   *pulled me from deep mud.*
> *He stood me up on a solid rock*
>   *to make sure I wouldn't slip.*
>   (Psalm 40:1–2 MSG)

David's song further encourages us to connect with the song God placed in our hearts, persevering even when the way is shrouded in mystery.

> *He taught me how to sing the latest God-song,*
>   *a praise-song to our God.*
> *More and more people are seeing this:*
>   *they enter the mystery,*
>   *abandoning themselves to God.*
>   (Psalm 40:3 MSG)

We offer encouragement from fellow writers who are listening for the music, the God-song to carry them into September and toward their goals.

"After a busy month with very little writing, I sat down this morning, set my timer, and wrote for 30 mins. It felt so good!! Now that everyone is back in school,

I feel life returning to a more routine rhythm. So, I'm praying for the Lord to help me fit writing into that routine!"—Mary

"I finished our ministry newsletter this week, and now I need to get back on track with my memoir writing and blog posting."—Rebecca

"I have been in a stalemate with my writing, but today I sat down and wrote over 1,000 words and finished the first chapter in my memoir! "—Julee

"Added a post to my webpage, actually emailed a friend inviting them to visit it, and posted an invitation on my Facebook page."—Teresa

OK, now it's your turn. What one small step are you going to take in your writing life today?

My prayer for the month

September 2023

SUNDAY	MONDAY	TUESDAY	WEDNESDAY
3	4	5	6
10	11	12	13
17	18	19	20
24	25	26	27

THURSDAY	FRIDAY	SATURDAY
	1	2
7	8	9
14	15	16
21	22	23
28	29	30

Notes for the Month

PLAN FOR THE MONTH

Key Focus

Goals and Action Steps

1.

2.

3.

WEEKLY ACTION PLAN

DATE: FROM _____ TO _____

- [ ] **SUNDAY**
- [ ] **MONDAY**
- [ ] **TUESDAY**
- [ ] **WEDNESDAY**
- [ ] **THURSDAY**
- [ ] **FRIDAY**
- [ ] **SATURDAY**

Weekly Focus

To-Dos

Notes

WEEKLY ACTION PLAN

DATE: FROM _____ TO _____

- [ ] **SUNDAY**
- [ ] **MONDAY**
- [ ] **TUESDAY**
- [ ] **WEDNESDAY**
- [ ] **THURSDAY**
- [ ] **FRIDAY**
- [ ] **SATURDAY**

Weekly Focus

To-Dos

- [ ]
- [ ]
- [ ]
- [ ]
- [ ]
- [ ]
- [ ]
- [ ]
- [ ]
- [ ]

Notes

WEEKLY ACTION PLAN

DATE: FROM _____ TO _____

- [ ] **SUNDAY**
- [ ] **MONDAY**
- [ ] **TUESDAY**
- [ ] **WEDNESDAY**
- [ ] **THURSDAY**
- [ ] **FRIDAY**
- [ ] **SATURDAY**

Weekly Focus

To-Dos

- [ ]
- [ ]
- [ ]
- [ ]
- [ ]
- [ ]
- [ ]
- [ ]
- [ ]
- [ ]

Notes

WEEKLY ACTION PLAN

DATE: FROM _____ TO _____

- [ ] **SUNDAY**
- [ ] **MONDAY**
- [ ] **TUESDAY**
- [ ] **WEDNESDAY**
- [ ] **THURSDAY**
- [ ] **FRIDAY**
- [ ] **SATURDAY**

Weekly Focus

To-Dos

Notes

WEEKLY ACTION PLAN

DATE: FROM _____ TO _____

- [ ] **SUNDAY**
- [ ] **MONDAY**
- [ ] **TUESDAY**
- [ ] **WEDNESDAY**
- [ ] **THURSDAY**
- [ ] **FRIDAY**
- [ ] **SATURDAY**

Weekly Focus

To-Dos

- [ ]
- [ ]
- [ ]
- [ ]
- [ ]
- [ ]
- [ ]
- [ ]
- [ ]
- [ ]

Notes

Notes

MONTH IN REVIEW

September

What worked well?

What didn't work well?

What am I celebrating?

What did I learn?

What am I grateful for?

Did I meet my goals? Do I need to adjust my goals for the next month?

> Writing isn't a skill that some people are born with and others aren't, like a gift for art or music. Writing is talking to someone else on paper. If you can think clearly, you can put what you think and what you know into writing.
>
> *William Zinsser*

Third Quarter in Review

July – August – September

It's time to review the third quarter as a whole.

Refer to the page titled "A Plan for My Writing Life" and to the quarter plan you filled out at the beginning of this quarter.

Use the "Third Quarter in Review" page to evaluate and reflect on the past quarter as you plan for the next.

Consider the following questions as you reflect:

- What worked well?
- What didn't work well?
- What are you celebrating?
- What did you learn?
- What are you grateful for?
- Did you meet your goals?
- Do you need to adjust your goals for the next quarter?

Make any adjustments you feel necessary to the plan for your writing life.

If you feel blocked or overwhelmed at any stage, stop and pray. Dig into *The Writer's Block Remedy Kit*. Its spiritual battle plan and soul-care remedies are designed for times when overwhelm hits and hope wanes. We want you to find joy and peace in your writing life.

THIRD QUARTER IN REVIEW

JULY
AUGUST
SEPTEMBER

What worked well?

What didn't work well?

What am I celebrating?

What did I learn?

What am I grateful for?

Did I meet my goals? Do I need to adjust my goals for the next quarter?

The Writer's Life Fourth Quarter *Planning*

The *Fourth* Quarter

October – November – December

It's time to identify your quarter plans for the next three months. Since you've built a strong foundation, planning for each quarter, month, and week is easier to achieve with confidence.

As you select your focus for the fourth quarter, refer to the page titled "A Plan for My Writing Life." Consider your plans for the next three months by answering this question: "What do I want to accomplish this quarter?" The goal that comes to mind will be your key focus.

Remember to pull out your "I Am a FlourishWriter" Scripture and affirmation to remind you why you started out on this journey. If you're feeling stuck or overwhelmed, refer to *The Writer's Block Remedy Kit* at the end of this planning guide.

What do I want to accomplish this quarter?

Select Goals and Action Steps for This Quarter

In light of your key focus for the quarter, brainstorm your goals and action steps. Use the space on the following page to note everything that comes to mind. Be sure to refer to your goal-planning maps. Remember the new writer who wants to create a novel. This is her goal for the year, but she is still learning how to write a novel. Her goal for the fourth quarter is to begin writing her novel. Her action steps are (1) prepare for NaNoWriMo in November, (2) schedule a four-day writing retreat in November, and (3) continue working on her draft in December. She likely will not complete the novel this year, but she will work consistently toward that goal.

As you brainstorm your action steps, these questions may be helpful:

- What do I need to know?
- What do I need to do?
- Are any actions dependent on other actions being completed first?
- Do I need to gather resources?
- What help do I need?

After you've brainstormed action steps, fill out your quarter plan. Write down your key focus for the quarter and your top one, two, or three goals, with accompanying action steps.

As you're working through this process, consider what you have going on for the next three months in your personal life. Doing so will give you realistic expectations about what you can accomplish in your writing life this quarter.

Brainstorm Action Steps

FOURTH QUARTER PLAN

OCTOBER
NOVEMBER
DECEMBER

Key Focus

GOAL 1	GOAL 2	GOAL 3
Action Steps	Action Steps	Action Steps
○	○	○
○	○	○
○	○	○
○	○	○
○	○	○
○	○	○
○	○	○

October

Oliver Burkeman observes, "The average human life span is absurdly, terrifyingly, insultingly short," about 4,000 weeks.

Why does 4,000 weeks sound so brief?

Think back to our launching place in *The Writer's Life Planning Guide*, Psalm 90:12: *Teach us to number our days, that we may gain a heart of wisdom.*

Since Moses asks God to teach us, surely we can learn this skill. Isn't that a relief? We can learn to number our days, to value the gift of time each day contains.

Even if we suspect our own ineptitude, God's power is available to us. God is at work in us "to will and to act in order to fulfill his good purpose" (Philippians 2:13).

The phrase "to will" in that Scripture catches my (Mindy's) eye. *Strong's Concordance* defines the Greek word as follows: "to be resolved or determined, wanting what is *best* by someone who is *ready* and *willing* to act."

You took a step of resolution and determination to become more intentional in your writing life. You've been at it for some months now. Yet here we are with three months remaining in the year. What a cornucopia of opportunity remains! 12 weeks. 91 days. 2,184 hours.

You've committed this year to learning, to making lasting progress, and to seeing real change—not at a rabbit's sprint, but with a tortoise's persistence, moving forward at a pace you can sustain for a lifetime.

You're designing a durable writing life built to last. This takes a resolved, determined act of will, tapping into God's power to fuel your next step . . . and the next and the next.

If you've been praying for perseverance, your writing life is quite possibly an answer. Crafting words to share with others is reminiscent less of microwave culture and more of the Slow Food movement. You're not serving up a frozen dinner. You're taking time to curate a meal of the freshest ingredients with sublime seasoning. Skill is gained during a long apprenticeship in which you keep showing up, ready to learn, ready to improve, ready to try again.

All your hope, all your vision, all your goals boil down to a simple question: "What are we doing today, God?"

Make a habit of asking this question every day. Be prepared for any answer. Some days the Spirit instructs through intense labor. Other days are for festive recreation. At times, we're invited to a luxurious nap with a belly full of pumpkin spice.

Ooh, ooh, can that be today, please?!

We are FlourishWriters, ready and willing to act, especially if it involves cinnamon, ginger, and nutmeg. Enjoy your October planning with a splash of aromatic spices.

My prayer for the month

October 2023

SUNDAY	MONDAY	TUESDAY	WEDNESDAY
1	2	3	4
8	9	10	11
15	16	17	18
22	23	24	25
29	30	31	

THURSDAY	FRIDAY	SATURDAY
5	6	7
12	13	14
19	20	21
26	27	28

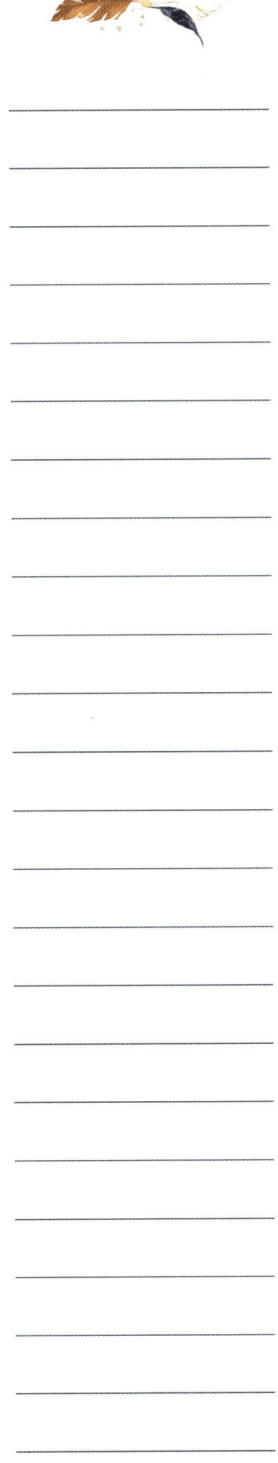

Notes for the Month

PLAN FOR THE MONTH

October

Key Focus

Goals and Action Steps

1.

2.

3.

WEEKLY ACTION PLAN

DATE: FROM _____ TO _____

- ☐ **SUNDAY**
- ☐ **MONDAY**
- ☐ **TUESDAY**
- ☐ **WEDNESDAY**
- ☐ **THURSDAY**
- ☐ **FRIDAY**
- ☐ **SATURDAY**

Weekly Focus

To-Dos

Notes

WEEKLY ACTION PLAN

DATE: FROM _____ TO _____

- [ ] **SUNDAY**

- [ ] **MONDAY**

- [ ] **TUESDAY**

- [ ] **WEDNESDAY**

- [ ] **THURSDAY**

- [ ] **FRIDAY**

- [ ] **SATURDAY**

Weekly Focus

To-Dos

- ○
- ○
- ○
- ○
- ○
- ○
- ○
- ○
- ○
- ○

Notes

WEEKLY ACTION PLAN

DATE: FROM _____ TO _____

- [ ] **SUNDAY**
- [ ] **MONDAY**
- [ ] **TUESDAY**
- [ ] **WEDNESDAY**
- [ ] **THURSDAY**
- [ ] **FRIDAY**
- [ ] **SATURDAY**

Weekly Focus

To-Dos

Notes

WEEKLY ACTION PLAN

DATE: FROM _____ TO _____

- [ ] **SUNDAY**
- [ ] **MONDAY**
- [ ] **TUESDAY**
- [ ] **WEDNESDAY**
- [ ] **THURSDAY**
- [ ] **FRIDAY**
- [ ] **SATURDAY**

Weekly Focus

To-Dos

- [ ]
- [ ]
- [ ]
- [ ]
- [ ]
- [ ]
- [ ]
- [ ]
- [ ]
- [ ]

Notes

WEEKLY ACTION PLAN

DATE: FROM _____ TO _____

☐ **SUNDAY**

☐ **MONDAY**

☐ **TUESDAY**

☐ **WEDNESDAY**

☐ **THURSDAY**

☐ **FRIDAY**

☐ **SATURDAY**

Weekly Focus

To-Dos

○
○
○
○
○
○
○
○
○
○

Notes

Notes

MONTH IN REVIEW

What worked well?

What didn't work well?

What am I celebrating?

What did I learn?

What am I grateful for?

Did I meet my goals? Do I need to adjust my goals for the next month?

> There is always the danger that we may just do the work for the sake of the work. This is where the respect and the love and the devotion come in—that we do it to God, to Christ, and that's why we try to do it as beautifully as possible.
>
> *Mother Teresa*

November

The writing life is like a tapestry woven of multicolored threads. We launch into a new project, designing the scene our tapestry will depict, believing it's our job to tell our writing projects what they will look like. Sometimes it works out like we intend. Sometimes we're left guessing at the picture that's forming.

When a creative endeavor isn't progressing as planned, we have several choices. Self-blame is one of my (Mindy's) favorites. I think, *Why isn't this darn thing working out?* Then I consider who or what is to blame and realize, *Maybe I didn't work hard enough or don't have the skills.*

Mired in disappointment, the next jump is to grasp for quick solutions: *I'll wake earlier to get in my writing time, purchase a new course (buying things always helps—lol), plan a writing retreat, something, anything to break out of this stalled-out place.*

Some of us are tempted to blame the situation. *I guess this wasn't my time. What did I expect with all the responsibilities I have right now? I'll have to quit and come back to my writing later.* Blaming ourselves or our situation doesn't lead us forward. It keeps us stuck. Resisting the current situation as it is causes no end of misery.

What if we become curious instead?

Years ago, I sat in the therapist's office with my husband, frustrated because we weren't making progress. We were stuck. Our counselor suggested that instead of blaming each other, we become curious about the other's position.

"Curiosity places you in an inquisitive frame of mind," he said. "You're more likely to find creative solutions from this place."

I didn't want to be curious. I wanted my husband to stop resisting me and get on board with my plan. Ha ha, no chance! The more I pressure my husband, the less he cooperates.

We do this with writing projects too, don't we? We feel resistance, so we apply more pressure. But there is a better way. When your plans aren't coming together, try curiosity. If the beautiful tapestry you envisioned isn't turning out like you hoped, suspend your judgment and take a look at what you see. It may not be what you expected, but what opportunities do you find?

Rather than blaming yourself or others, allow curiosity to search for a creative step forward. You won't see opportunities when you're fed up with the current situation. Breathe a prayer of acceptance and ask these three gentle questions.

- Where do I find myself?
- What is this situation telling me?
- What alternatives do I see?

The present moment invites you to show up, inquisitive and attentive. One thing you have permission to resist is hopelessness. Futility is the nemesis of many a writer, but when you're committed to sharing the Spirit-breathed message on your heart, part of the job description is active resistance against forces of despair designed to steal your voice and place you in solitary confinement.

We won't let this happen, no matter what is working or *not* working in your writing life right now. Check in with your spiritual battle plan and soul-care remedies in *The Writer's Block Remedy Kit*.

"Is anything too difficult for the Lord" (Genesis 18:14 NASB)? What do you say? Take all the time you need to process your answers to the three gentle questions above, then go back to the loom, pick up the shuttle, and return to your weaving of words. We can't wait to see the tapestry only you can weave.

My prayer for the month

November 2023

SUNDAY	MONDAY	TUESDAY	WEDNESDAY
			1
5	6	7	8
12	13	14	15
19	20	21	22
26	27	28	29

THE WRITER'S LIFE PLANNING GUIDE

THURSDAY	FRIDAY	SATURDAY
2	3	4
9	10	11
16	17	18
23	24	25
30		

Notes for the Month

PLAN FOR THE MONTH

Key Focus

Goals and Action Steps

1.

2.

3.

WEEKLY ACTION PLAN

DATE: FROM _____ TO _____

- [ ] **SUNDAY**
- [ ] **MONDAY**
- [ ] **TUESDAY**
- [ ] **WEDNESDAY**
- [ ] **THURSDAY**
- [ ] **FRIDAY**
- [ ] **SATURDAY**

Weekly Focus

To-Dos

- [ ]
- [ ]
- [ ]
- [ ]
- [ ]
- [ ]
- [ ]
- [ ]
- [ ]
- [ ]

Notes

WEEKLY ACTION PLAN

DATE: FROM _____ TO _____

- [ ] **SUNDAY**
- [ ] **MONDAY**
- [ ] **TUESDAY**
- [ ] **WEDNESDAY**
- [ ] **THURSDAY**
- [ ] **FRIDAY**
- [ ] **SATURDAY**

Weekly Focus

To-Dos

Notes

WEEKLY ACTION PLAN

DATE: FROM _____ TO _____

- [ ] **SUNDAY**
- [ ] **MONDAY**
- [ ] **TUESDAY**
- [ ] **WEDNESDAY**
- [ ] **THURSDAY**
- [ ] **FRIDAY**
- [ ] **SATURDAY**

Weekly Focus

To-Dos

- [ ]
- [ ]
- [ ]
- [ ]
- [ ]
- [ ]
- [ ]
- [ ]
- [ ]
- [ ]

Notes

WEEKLY ACTION PLAN

DATE: FROM _____ TO _____

- [ ] **SUNDAY**
- [ ] **MONDAY**
- [ ] **TUESDAY**
- [ ] **WEDNESDAY**
- [ ] **THURSDAY**
- [ ] **FRIDAY**
- [ ] **SATURDAY**

Weekly Focus

To-Dos

Notes

WEEKLY ACTION PLAN

DATE: FROM _____ TO _____

☐ **SUNDAY**

☐ **MONDAY**

☐ **TUESDAY**

☐ **WEDNESDAY**

☐ **THURSDAY**

☐ **FRIDAY**

☐ **SATURDAY**

Weekly Focus

To-Dos

Notes

Notes

MONTH IN REVIEW

What worked well?

What didn't work well?

What am I celebrating?

What did I learn?

What am I grateful for?

Did I meet my goals? Do I need to adjust my goals for the next month?

> *Observe each week and month emerge, holding the tension between the plan and reality, viewing challenges as growth opportunities rather than dead ends. A growth mindset sees disruption through the lens of learning.*
>
> — *Mindy and Jenny*

December

We arrive at the destination and realize it's not a destination after all but a place to pause and reflect on where we've come from, where we are, and where we're going. When you say yes to the writing life, you step into a river that has been flowing for thousands of years. Much of the time, the river flows as expected, but then raging floodwaters arrive without warning. You look about for others in the river, hoping to grab hold of a hand for stability.

Are you feeling lost or found in your journey? As I (Mindy) read the Parable of the Lost Son in the fifteenth chapter of Luke, I notice it follows the Parable of the Lost Sheep and the Parable of the Lost Coin. With the sheep and the coin, someone else seeks them out and comes to the rescue. But with the son, he has to use his legs to make his own way home.

The beginning of verse 17 catches my eye: "When he came to his senses . . ." (Luke 15:17a).

Rebecca, a sister FlourishWriter, shares when she "came to her senses" with the decision to scale back her goals: "After Mindy's encouragement and good direction, my yearly goal has changed from having my book done to having the *rough draft* of it done. Thank you all for the 'cheering on' that takes place in FlourishWriters. The promise in Psalm 32:8 buoys my spirit as I continue to follow His lead in this project. Funny how we have to keep 'coming to our senses' when we forget that it's *'Not by might nor by power, but by My Spirit,' says the Lord Almighty* (Zechariah 4:6)."

We come to our senses and realize we are one small voice empowered by a mighty calling to speak out with hope and joy to a hurting world. We grasp the hand of God and the hands of our faithful companions in the journey.

Jill says, "The most significant blessing I have received from being part of FlourishWriters has been learning to discern the Shepherd's voice in my writing life. With the encouragement of Mindy, Jenny, and fellow writers, I have discovered

- how to allow God to use my personal experiences to encourage others through the written word,

- how to focus in on the messages that God has put on my heart for that purpose,
- and how to take a stand against the forces of distraction and discouragement.

"I have received abundant practical information and tools, but my favorite thing about this gathering of writers is how it prepares our hearts to answer God's call with courage and in His strength, so we can open our hands and say, 'God, these writing hands are yours. Lead them in your wonderful way.'"

We arrive at the end of this year and look back with gratitude for the Shepherd who guides us to still waters and navigates us through river rapids. We receive mercy for where we find ourselves, even if it isn't where we thought we would be. We grab hold of hope for the future, determined to keep going even though the only certainty is that we can't predict exactly what it will look like when we get there.

Thank you for journeying with us, dear friends. At this month's end, enjoy a time of reflection as you complete the "Year in Review" page and say, "God, these writing hands are yours. Lead them in your wonderful way."

My prayer for the month

December 2023

SUNDAY	MONDAY	TUESDAY	WEDNESDAY
3	4	5	6
10	11	12	13
17	18	19	20
24 / 31	25	26	27

THURSDAY	FRIDAY	SATURDAY
	1	2
7	8	9
14	15	16
21	22	23
28	29	30

Notes for the Month

PLAN FOR THE MONTH

Key Focus

Goals and Action Steps

1.

2.

3.

WEEKLY ACTION PLAN

DATE: FROM _____ TO _____

- [ ] **SUNDAY**
- [ ] **MONDAY**
- [ ] **TUESDAY**
- [ ] **WEDNESDAY**
- [ ] **THURSDAY**
- [ ] **FRIDAY**
- [ ] **SATURDAY**

Weekly Focus

To-Dos

Notes

WEEKLY ACTION PLAN

DATE: FROM _____ TO _____

- [ ] **SUNDAY**
- [ ] **MONDAY**
- [ ] **TUESDAY**
- [ ] **WEDNESDAY**
- [ ] **THURSDAY**
- [ ] **FRIDAY**
- [ ] **SATURDAY**

Weekly Focus

To-Dos

Notes

WEEKLY ACTION PLAN

DATE: FROM _____ TO _____

- [ ] **SUNDAY**

- [ ] **MONDAY**

- [ ] **TUESDAY**

- [ ] **WEDNESDAY**

- [ ] **THURSDAY**

- [ ] **FRIDAY**

- [ ] **SATURDAY**

Weekly Focus

To-Dos

Notes

WEEKLY ACTION PLAN

DATE: FROM _____ TO _____

- [ ] **SUNDAY**
- [ ] **MONDAY**
- [ ] **TUESDAY**
- [ ] **WEDNESDAY**
- [ ] **THURSDAY**
- [ ] **FRIDAY**
- [ ] **SATURDAY**

Weekly Focus

To-Dos

- [ ]
- [ ]
- [ ]
- [ ]
- [ ]
- [ ]
- [ ]
- [ ]
- [ ]
- [ ]

Notes

WEEKLY ACTION PLAN

DATE: FROM _____ TO _____

- [ ] **SUNDAY**
- [ ] **MONDAY**
- [ ] **TUESDAY**
- [ ] **WEDNESDAY**
- [ ] **THURSDAY**
- [ ] **FRIDAY**
- [ ] **SATURDAY**

Weekly Focus

To-Dos

Notes

Notes

MONTH IN REVIEW

What worked well?

What didn't work well?

What am I celebrating?

What did I learn?

What am I grateful for?

Did I meet my goals? Do I need to adjust my goals for the next month?

> *It always seems impossible until it's done.*
>
> — *Nelson Mandela*

Fourth Quarter in Review

October – November – December

It's time to review the fourth quarter as a whole.

Refer to the page titled "A Plan for My Writing Life" and to the quarter plan you filled out at the beginning of this quarter.

Use the "Fourth Quarter in Review" page to evaluate and reflect on the past quarter.

Consider the following questions as you reflect:

- What worked well?
- What didn't work well?
- What are you celebrating?
- What did you learn?
- What are you grateful for?
- Did you meet your goals?

Make any adjustments you feel necessary to the plan for your writing life.

If you feel blocked or overwhelmed at any stage, stop and pray. Dig into *The Writer's Block Remedy Kit*. Its spiritual battle plan and soul-care remedies are designed for times when overwhelm hits and hope wanes. We want you to find joy and peace in your writing life.

FOURTH QUARTER REVIEW

OCTOBER
NOVEMBER
DECEMBER

What worked well?

What didn't work well?

What am I celebrating?

What did I learn?

What am I grateful for?

Did I meet my goals?

The Writer's Life Year in *Review*

You Made It. Woohoo! You made it to the end of the year. You may have stumbled through some valleys, but hopefully you scaled a few mountains too. It may not have been pretty (or maybe it was!), yet you set off on this journey with a fire in your belly to share your message. You chose to invest in yourself and your writing life. You put in the time to seek vision, clarify your why, and make steady progress on your writing goals.

We're proud of you and all you've accomplished. Do you hear us cheering?!

Here you are at the end but also at a new beginning. You said yes to the call to write, and God is your strength. This is a lifelong process, one that you will walk out for many years to come.

We ask God to bless you in your next steps as He reveals His purpose in your writing:

> *We have become his poetry, a re-created people that will fulfill the destiny he has given each of us, for we are joined to Jesus, the Anointed One. Even before we were born, God planned in advance our destiny and the good works we would do to fulfill it!* (Ephesians 2:10 TPT)

Take a moment to reflect on where you were when you started out on this writing journey and on where you are now. On the pages that follow, write out your thoughts as you review the completion of this year.

You have space to answer these questions as you reflect:

- What went well this year?
- What are you thankful for?
- What gave you energy and joy?
- What goals did you achieve this year?
- What challenges did you face?
- What lessons did you learn?

Reflect on Your Year

Congratulations! And welcome to your end-of-year reflection.

What went well this year?

What am I thankful for?

What gave me energy and joy?

What goals did I achieve?

What challenges did I face?

What lessons did I learn?

Notes

The Writer's Block *Remedy* Kit

Your *Spiritual* Battle Plan and *Soul-Care* Remedies

The Writer's Block *Remedy* Kit

Everyone faces writer's block or at least writer's uncertainty at some point in the writing process.

Voices of doubt make us question our goals. "What was I thinking?"

Confusion settles in when we lose our way in the writing. "Where am I?"

Or the busyness of life derails our goals. "I have no time!"

We don't want you to give up on the dream of a writing life!

That's why we created *The Writer's Block Remedy Kit* and stocked it with our best writer's remedies.

- The *spiritual battle plan* addresses the lies and limiting beliefs that hold you back. Strengthen your resolve with the truth of God's Word.

- The *soul-care remedies* help you overcome writer's block through prayer, worship, and a change of routine. When overwhelm hits and creativity is gone, take a break!

- A beautiful collection of Scripture art prints nourish your heart and mind with encouraging truths to keep you writing. Access your free download here: https://www.flourishwriters.com/writersblockremedykit.

My *Spiritual* Battle Plan

In Ephesians chapter 2, we see how God rescued us from death by making us alive in Christ. We are saved by His grace. He created us as a masterpiece, a poem, a song to praise His majesty.

What a thrilling promise! What hope!

The Master Creator lovingly fashioned you in His image. You are fearfully and wonderfully made (Psalm 139:14). He designed you with careful thought and imagination. He stands back and marvels at His creation and calls you blessed.

Listen to the words of the Lord: *Fear not, for I have redeemed you; I have called you by name, you are mine* (Isaiah 43:1 ESV).

Selah. Pause and think of this. The God of the universe promises, *I have called you by name.* Imagine how your name sounds on His lips. He says, *You are mine.*

Choosing to grow in your writing life takes a step of faith. In the writing process, you will learn about yourself and about God. Even if your book topic is not overtly spiritual, it's going to take profound perseverance to get it out of your head and onto the page. Your testimony will become a light shining forth to reveal Jesus' redeeming power to others.

Does Satan like this?

Absolutely not.

He will do everything in his power to thwart this revelation. There is a cosmic battle for your story. It's a battle that God has already won, but you must partner with Him to see the victory.

Building a writing life requires daily yielding to Holy Spirit, pressing in close to the comfort and shelter of His wings. We have provided several strategies to help you find shelter in God's protection as you share your message. Writer's block be gone!

We begin with your position, your ponderings, and your prayers.

Position Yourself *Close* to God

As you write, stay close to God. Intimacy with the Father is the best shield against our enemy. One major barrier between us and God is poor relationships with other people. If we close our hearts to others, we close our hearts to God (Matthew 25:40–46).

> *Whoever claims to love God yet hates a brother or sister is a liar. For whoever does not love their brother and sister, whom they have seen, cannot love God, whom they have not seen. (1 John 4:20)*

As John Bevere teaches in *The Bait of Satan*, offense in our hearts against another is to take Satan's bait. When we allow unforgiveness or bitterness to grow in our hearts, we are drawn away from the shelter of God's wings. Ask God to help you keep your heart open to others; however, use discernment if you are in a relationship characterized by dishonor or manipulation. If necessary, get help to be safe. Healthy boundaries are critical.

When God shows us how we have distanced ourselves from Him by holding offense against others, we repent and give the situation into His care, which opens our hearts once again. Having open hearts enables us to hear God's voice more clearly.

> *If you say, "The Lord is my refuge," and you make the Most High your dwelling, no harm will overtake you, no disaster will come near your tent. (Psalm 91:9)*

An example prayer for inviting God to open your heart follows:

God, I invite you to search me and reveal my deepest thoughts. Although you're acquainted with my heart and what I harbor, I'm tempted to hide. Without your help, I don't know my own heart. Examine me and let me know what you find in my deepest thoughts. You don't condemn me. No, you love me and want me to be free. Help me accept what you see in my unveiled heart. I don't want to hide from you. I desire to open my heart to your bold love so I may know the joy of your presence.

Tune into Your *Ponderings*

As you engage in the process of writing, pay attention to your ponderings. What are you thinking about? Is your heart heavy or hopeful? Satan is the Accuser. He desires to fill your thoughts with lies about who you are and who God is.

> *Finally, brothers and sisters, whatever is true, whatever is noble, whatever is right, whatever is pure, whatever is lovely, whatever is admirable—if anything is excellent or praiseworthy—think about such things.* (Philippians 4:8)

Ask God to help you be aware of your thoughts. Allow Holy Spirit to help you recognize when you are assailed by lies.

Our mind is a battleground. As soon as we quiet ourselves to focus on God, we are besieged by swirling thoughts. The last thing Satan wants is for us to settle in for a rich conversation with our Father. Knowing that the battle is real, we invite God to take every thought captive, to settle our minds by inviting clarity and focus (2 Corinthians 10:5). We ask the Lord to remove confusion, distraction, or double-mindedness from us.

An example prayer for inviting God to take your thoughts captive follows:

> Lord, you created my mind and called it good. At times, I feel that my thoughts betray me, but I know you can help me focus and take every thought captive. I repent for my pride and rebellion that fight against you. Jesus, I long to be submitted to you completely, to be obedient to you even in my thoughts. I place myself in your capable hands and invite you to be Lord over my mind.

One of our favorite declarations for renewing the mind is *The Father's Love Letter*, which you can find at www.fathersloveletter.com.

Seek *Perseverance* in Prayer

Staying connected to God through prayer is not just a good idea—it's a necessity. Prayer is not only talking to God but also listening. Keeping the prayer channels open enables you to receive messages from Holy Spirit rather than the Accuser. Praying Scripture will build up your mind and heart with truth.

> *God can do anything, you know—far more than you could ever imagine or guess or request in your wildest dreams! He does it not by pushing us around but by working within us, his Spirit deeply and gently within us.* (Ephesians 3:20 MSG)

Receive this Scripture-paraphrased declaration as a blessing for your identity in Christ:

> You are beautiful and you are beloved. God has blessed you with His love. God smiled on the day He created you. . . . Your world needs you. You bring something to your family that no other person has. They need the gifts you bring. Your family would not be complete without you. Others in your circle need the deposit that God has placed in your life. (Sylvia Gunter and Arthur Burk, *Blessing Your Spirit* [Father's Business Publishing, 2006], p. 2)

God loves to receive our prayers and declarations. He also desires to speak. God asks us to pay attention, to be silent and give Him a chance to reply (Job 33:31). He desires to answer our questions.

An example prayer for inviting God to speak to you follows:

> I'm expectant you'll speak to me, Jesus. I hope to experience a new way of hearing your voice and recognizing the evidence of your fingerprints in my life. Help me reject the Accuser's condemnation that tries to weigh me down with despair and doubt. Thank you, God, for drawing near to me and whispering your truth into my mind and heart.

Fuel Your *Determination*

The writing process may be profoundly challenging. Although difficulties are unpleasant, a psalmist highlights the value of persevering through hardship: *It is good for me that I was afflicted, that I might learn your statutes* (Psalm 119:71 ESV).

When God calls us to write, we respond with hope. It's discomforting to discover that there may be an element of frustration, despair, or hopelessness in the challenge. Bible verses that talk about finding life through death and growth through affliction are not most people's favorites. Yet, it appears God is more interested in your heart and your growth than in your ease.

For some reason, growth is rarely achieved without some measure of discomfort or even outright pain. Consider a baby's birth, cutting teeth, learning to walk, limbs that ache during a growth spurt. God knows this is the case, so He provides relief in His Word.

> *This is my comfort in my affliction, that your promise gives me life.* (Psalm 119:50 ESV)

Alright, we admit that pain is part of growth. Writing projects are rarely pain-free. So if affliction is coming, how do we endure these times of trial and valleys of despair? To put it in perspective, let's consider Job, the righteous man from Uz. How does Job remain steadfast? How does he persevere in the face of anguish?

Job treasures God, and he is treasured by God. Job's life is sustained by his heart for the Lord.

> *For where your treasure is, there your heart will be also.* (Matthew 6:21)

When destruction is loosed in his life, Job discovers he has an unshakable foundation beneath his feet: the Rock of his salvation. Despite mounting afflictions, Job discovers he has a fire in the pit of his belly. It will not be quenched by any suffering the enemy launches against him. In fact, his determination is galvanized by affliction.

We ask God to bless you with a steadfast spirit as you persevere in your writing project. May your determination be fueled by His strength, sufficient for the task at hand. *You can do it because He can do it.*

Prepare Your *Spiritual* Battle Plan

Your tailored spiritual battle plan and practical soul-care remedies will help you thrive during the writing process. God renews and strengthens us in many ways, not solely through traditional spiritual practices, but also through physical refreshment. May you experience Jesus as your Savior in new and marvelous ways—body, soul, and spirit—during your writing process.

Now let's get your remedy kit organized through the reflection steps that follow.

Read Ephesians 2:10 in several different Bible translations and ponder God's message there for you as a writer.

We have become his poetry, a re-created people that will fulfill the destiny he has given each of us, for we are joined to Jesus, the Anointed One. Even before we were born, God planned in advance our destiny and the good works we would do to fulfill it! (Ephesians 2:10 TPT)

Write a prayer dedicating your writing process to the Lord, recording it in the space below.

STEP 2

Writers are often attacked by lies that become limiting beliefs. What lies tend to attack you regarding your identity—that is, who you are as a person? Write each lie in the left column of the chart below.

In the right column, respond to each lie with a truth God says about you. Reference a Bible story showing someone overcoming the lie, or cite a Scripture that comes to mind or that you find by using a reference Bible.

One row of the chart is filled in as an example.

Lies about my Identity	Truth + Scripture Reference
I never finish what I start.	With God's strength, I can do anything. *He will also keep you firm to the end, so that you will be blameless on the day of our Lord Jesus Christ* (1 Corinthians 1:8).

STEP 3

What lies attack you regarding your story or the topic you're writing about? Write each lie in the left column of the chart below.

In the right column, write the corresponding truths God says about your writing project. Reference Bible stories showing people overcoming the lies, or cite Scriptures that come to mind or that you find by using a reference Bible.

One row of the chart is filled in as an example.

Lies about my Story or Topic	Scriptural Truth
Nothing will happen with my writing. It will just be a waste of time and words.	Maybe the process is more about me than for others. I just need to obey; the results are in God's hands. *The horse is made ready for the day of battle, but victory rests with the Lord* (Proverbs 21:31).

STEP 4

What lies tend to attack you regarding your ability as a writer? Write each lie in the left column of the chart below.

In the right column, write corresponding truths God says about your writing ability. Reference Bible stories showing people overcoming the lies, or cite Scriptures that come to mind or that you find by using a reference Bible.

One row of the chart is filled in as an example.

Lies about my ability as a Writer	Scriptural Truth
I'm not going to be able to explain everything so people can understand it.	Holy Spirit is the great communicator. As long as I'm doing my part to the best of my ability in obedience to the Lord, He is the one who creates understanding. *The Advocate, the Holy Spirit, whom the Father will send in my name, will teach you all things and will remind you of everything I have said to you (John 14:26).*

A Helpful Tip — Make index cards or print pages with the verses of truth you found, and post them in a prominent place. Or make a flip-book of the verses, to read when you need a reinforcement of truth to combat the lies. This ammunition against the lies of the enemy is part of your spiritual battle plan.

Prepare Your *Soul-Care* Remedies

Reflect on any other ways you are usually attacked when you begin to write. Ask God, "How can I respond from a place of strength in You? What can I do when these lies come after me?"

[ ]

The enemy has plans to take us down, but Christ has defeated him. When you prepare your spiritual battle plan and soul-care remedies, you find shelter under the wings of the Almighty. Let us remember this bold promise:

> *He gives strength to the weary and increases the power of the weak. Even youths grow tired and weary, and young men stumble and fall; but those who hope in the Lord will renew their strength. They will soar on wings like eagles; they will run and not grow weary, they will walk and not be faint.* (Isaiah 40:29–31)

The Hebrew word here translated "weary" means "physical fatigue from lack of bread." Consider the Lord's Prayer in Matthew chapter 6, where Jesus instructs us to pray for our daily bread. This plea for nourishment is also a request for divine provision in all things. God supplies the strength we need to walk according to His will. He is our strength when we are weak. He is the only Savior worthy of our trust. May you press in close to His heartbeat for you.

STEP 2

Now consider practical steps you can take to fight back when your writing life is under attack. We have provided ideas in the concept map below.

STEP 3

Referring to the ideas on the previous page for inspiration, use the blank concept map below to record your specific soul-care remedies. Think through what works for you personally. What refreshes you? What helps you to release your burdens to the Lord? What makes you smile? These are your remedies for writer's block.

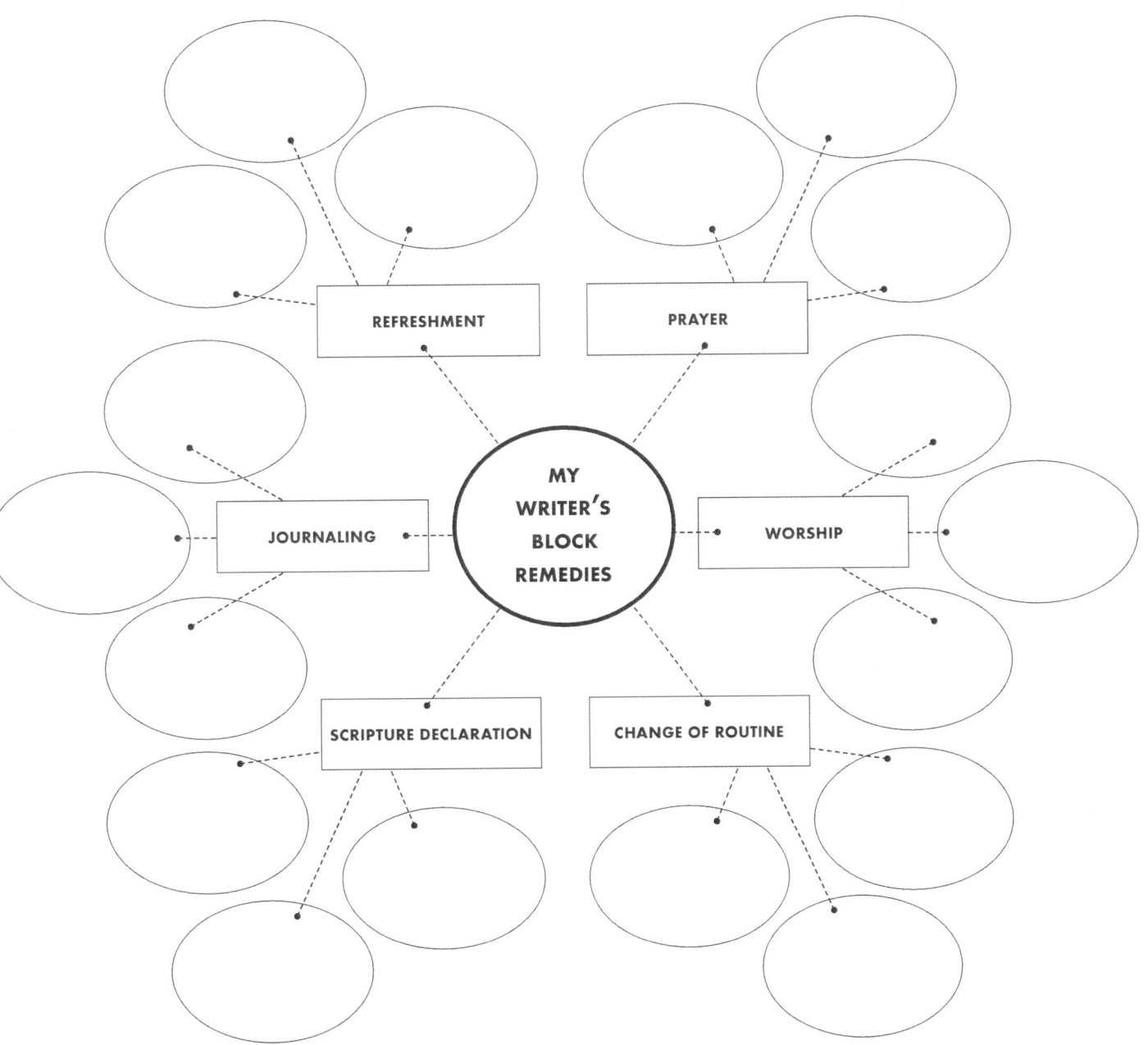

Do you have a *message* on your heart you wish to write?

If you have a story that needs to get from your heart to the page, you've found the right book. *The Flourish Writers Guide to Writing: Crafting Your Nonfiction Message One Step at a Time* equips you to

- **CLARIFY** and prioritize your ideas so you know what project to start first;
- **ORGANIZE** your writing projects (*even if you're not a natural planner*);
- **PRACTICE** writing techniques to help you complete the first draft;
- **GROW** as a self-editor capable of producing a polished manuscript; and
- **SHOW UP** with confidence as you share your words with others.

The *Guide to Writing* Masterclass Collection provides written and video video instruction to help you master the essential skills of the writing craft. It's all designed for aspiring and working writers to grow in the craft of nonfiction writing.

Get your keyboard fired up as you engage in hands-on learning with clear explanations and easy-to-follow examples provided in the 170-page guidebook. Checklists and practice exercises teach you to manage your writing projects from idea to done.

While most organizations focus almost entirely on craft or productivity, Mindy and Jenny have created a unique offering where your artistry will blossom, your soul will thrive, and your writing will flourish . . . one story at a time.

—**ALLEN ARNOLD,** Award-winning author of *The Story of With*

FlourishWriters not only teaches you the craft of writing, it helps cultivate the heart of Jesus in everything you do. Oh, how I wish I had FlourishWriters when I started writing so many years ago!

—**JOANNA WEAVER,** Award-winning author of *Having a Mary Heart in a Martha World*

Find out more at www.flourishwritersguidetowriting.com

If you need anything at all, we're ready to help!

You can email us at
info@flourishgathering.com

or find us on Facebook
@theflourishwriterscommunity

flourishwriters.com

Made in the USA
Middletown, DE
06 January 2023

21584436R00142